THIRD EDITION

REAL ESTATE ETHICS

GOOD ETHICS = GOOD BUSINESS

William H. Pivar & Donald L. Harlan

Real Estate
Education Company
a division of Dearborn Financial Publishing, Inc.

While a great deal of care has been taken to provide accurate and current information, the ideas, suggestions, general principles and conclusions presented in this book are subject to local, state and federal laws and regulations, court cases and any revisions of same. The reader is thus urged to consult legal counsel regarding any points of law—this publication should not be used as a substitute for competent legal advice.

Publisher: Carol L. Luitjens
Associate Development Editor: Kristen Short
Project Editor: Debra M. Hall
Art and Design Manager: Lucy Jenkins
Cover Design: Elizandro Carrington

Published by Real Estate Education Company®,
a division of Dearborn Financial Publishing, Inc.®
155 N. Wacker Drive
Chicago, IL 60606-1719
1-800-621-9621

Printed in the United States of America.

98 99 00 01 02 10 9 8 7 6 5 4

Library of Congress Cataloging-in-Publication Data

Pivar, William H.
    Real estate ethics : good ethics=good business / William H. Pivar
& Donald L. Harlan.—3rd ed.
        p. cm.
    Includes bibliographical references and index.
    ISBN 0-7931-1236-2
    1. Real estate agents—Professional ethics. 2. Real estate
business. 3. Business ethics. 4. Real property. I. Harlan,
Donald L. II. Title.
HD1382.P58 1995   95-9476
    174'.4—dc20   CIP

Contents

Chapter 3 Responsibilities to the Buyer   47

Disclosure + Fairness = A Satisfied Buyer

Chapter 4 Responsibilities to the General Public   75

Regard for Community and Profession = Ethical, Sound Business Practices

Chapter 5 Responsibilities to Other Licensees   95

Practicing the Golden Rule = Benefits for All

Case Studies

Preface

In recent years, our society has been experiencing a moral reawakening. People are beginning to examine their actions not in terms of what is legal but in terms of what is right.

In real estate, we have long been aware of our ethical duties, but questions of what is right or wrong are becoming more complex. This book was written to help real estate licensees analyze and understand their ethical relationships with others; it can do nothing to change a reader's character. However, if you are like the majority of real estate professionals, people who strive to be responsible, forthright, loyal, honest and fair in their dealings, who keep their promises and are respectful and show concern regarding the rights and feelings of others, then this book will remind you of your ethical duties and help you in making ethical decisions in your daily life.

Many state licensing agencies, real estate boards and reviewers suggested specific problem areas. Most of the cases and ethics questions presented in this book are based on real situations.

Questions and the authors' recommendations at the end of each chapter are offered so that you can consider your own solutions based on ethical considerations and to aid you in analyzing those solutions.

The ethical and legal opinions expressed are those of the authors and are intended only as guidelines for ethical conduct. They do not necessarily illustrate the only proper course of action in any given circumstance.

We would like to hear from you if you disagree or have additional thoughts as to ethical solutions, or have any interesting ethical cases or dilemmas for inclusion in future editions of this book.

Acknowledgments

We would like to express our sincere gratitude to the National Association of REALTORS® and their subsidiary groups, as well as to the many local boards of REALTORS® and state licensing agencies who provided assistance in preparing this book. We also would like to thank all who encouraged us on this project.

Special thanks to our reviewers: Ruth Blank, Palm Springs, California; Frank Kovats, Paramus, New Jersey; John Kokus, Jr., PhD, Washington, D.C.; Mark L. Friedman, South Portland, Maine; Karen Otrupchak, Ocean, New Jersey; Mary Koveny, Naperville, Illinois; and John A. Spicuglia, Hudson, Florida.

Note: A REALTOR® is a member of the National Association of REALTORS®, who thereby subscribes to its Code of Ethics.

About the Authors

Dr. William H. Pivar has served as a private, corporate and government attorney specializing in real estate and has worked as a consultant for some of the nation's largest real estate firms and developers.

He has served as an arbitrator with the Federal Mediation and Conciliation Service and the American Arbitration Association.

From 1971 to 1994, Dr. Pivar served as the real estate coordinator and professor of business education at College of the Desert, a California community college in Palm Desert where he is now Professor Emeritus. In 1994, Dr. Pivar was designated California Real Estate Educator of the Year.

Dr. Pivar's other 28 book titles include *Power Real Estate Listing, Power Real Estate Selling, Power Real Estate Letters, Simplified Classifieds, Classified Secrets, California Real Estate Practice, California Real Estate Law* and *Real Estate Exam Guide*.

Donald L. Harlan, CRE, CCIM, CRB, GRI, DREI, ABR, is a manager and the broker of the brokerage/consulting division of Harlan, Lyons & Associates, LLC. He has been active in all phases of residential and commercial real estate as a broker and consultant in the Denver area since 1971.

Mr. Harlan has served in many leadership roles for various REALTOR® groups, which include chairman, Professional Standards Education Subcommittee, Interpretations and Procedures Subcommittee, Specialty Practices Study Group, National Association of REALTORS®; president, cochairman of the Professional Standards/Risk Reduction Committee, Senior Instructor for Ethics and Professional Practices, Colorado Association of REALTORS®; and president, Denver Board of REALTORS®.

Mr. Harlan and his partner Gail Lyons—experts in agency practice—have coauthored numerous articles and six books on all aspects of real estate. They also have presented seminars and trained more than 35,000 REALTORS® throughout the United States, Canada and Eastern Europe.

1. Understanding Ethics

Real Estate Ethics = Doing What Is Right

Ethics Defined

The word *ethics* derives from the Greek *ethikos*, meaning moral, and *ethos*, meaning character. In a standard textbook definition, ethics is "a branch of philosophy that deals with the values of human life in a coherent, systematic and scientific manner." The *Oxford English Dictionary* defines ethics as "the department of study concerned with the principles of human duty" and "the rules or conduct recognized in certain associations or departments of human life."

You will not find universal agreement among philosophers as to what, exactly, is ethically right. Immanuel Kant believed that what is right is based on pure reason. Moral philosophers believe right to be that which will produce the greatest good. Religious philosophers believe that right is determined by the will of God, and wrong is that which is contrary to God's will.

For the purpose of this book, we will use Albert Schweitzer's definition:

1

"Ethics is the name we give to our concern for good behavior. We feel an obligation to consider not only our own personal well-being but also that of others and of human society as a whole."

Dr. Schweitzer applied this idea of "duty beyond the group" to all of humanity. He believed that the ultimate goal of ethics is the fullest measure of justice for all. If we were to condense the philosophy of Dr. Schweitzer into three words, they would be _regard for others_.

When we discuss ethics, we are therefore not dealing with a set of hard-and-fast scientific precepts, but rather with subjective behavior. The Golden Rule, "Do unto others as you would have others do unto you," provides us with a basic test of ethical conduct.

You can easily determine whether a course of action is ethical simply by asking, "Would I want someone else to act in this manner toward me?" Failure to apply the Golden Rule will result in two separate standards of ethics—a double standard. One is how you treat others, the second is how you expect others to treat you. Application of the Golden Rule in your daily life can make these two separate standards one.

A Phoenix area real estate broker, Irv Also, has distilled ethics into six words. The first phrase is _don't hurt anyone_. Hurt can be physical, mental, moral or monetary. If you somehow, whether accidentally, unknowingly, inadvertently or even deliberately, hurt someone, the second phrase takes over: _make it right_. While simple, these six words capture the essence of the Golden Rule.

Success in Real Estate

Many real estate firms give recognition to top producers of sales and listings. While success in sales and listings is important and should be recognized, we should not fail to recognize those who have expended their efforts to better meet the needs of others by completing educational courses and obtaining professional designations as well as those who have given of themselves by serving in leadership roles in maintaining and raising the professionalism of the real estate industry.

One danger of an overemphasis on financial rewards is that it could lead some real estate licensees to evaluate customers and clients solely on the basis of what the licensee can get from them. An apparent overemphasis on dollars could lead new licensees to the conclusion that any means to the desired end is acceptable.

Ethical Capitalism

When asked why they chose real estate as a profession, students in real estate license preparation classes often answer, "Money." Real estate ads for salespeople often stress dollars and not that real estate allows a person to perform an interesting and rewarding service by meeting the needs of people in a professional capacity. Certainly we expect to be adequately rewarded for success, and money is important in our society, but the first concern of a professional is to meet the needs of the client and the public in a proper and ethical manner. If we succeed in meeting the needs of others, our financial aspirations will also be met.

Ethics does not have to be incompatible with capitalism; *profit* is not a dirty word. You may ask why you should be ethical in business. If you are pragmatic, you will see a practical benefit in ethical behavior. Most real estate professionals will tell you that referrals are an important element in their success. Owners who are referred to real estate licensees are presold on the integrity and professionalism of the licensees. Buyers who come to them because of referrals know that the licensee will work hard to find a property that best meets their needs and will do so in an open and honest manner. These sellers and buyers come to these real estate professionals because people they respect and trust also respect and trust these real estate professionals.

Emerson wrote, "Virtue is the business of the universe." You will find that good ethics (virtue) is good business.

Real estate is an aggressive profession in which you should compete vigorously. In fact, vigorous competition will lead to serving the public's needs better. Applying the Golden Rule does not mean you should allow someone else to make a sale in the hope that he or she might let you make the next one.

Ethics is personal and applies to you. Because it is personal, as an ethical person you are not required to place implicit trust in others. You have no control over the conduct of others, only over yourself. As an example, if you were asked to sign a written agreement that had been verbally explained to you, it would not be unethical to read the document carefully prior to signing it.

Ethical versus Legal

Students often express concern that ethics deals with the way things ought to be, which is not always seen as practical in our society. They also have difficulties distinguishing between what is ethical and what is legal, two completely separate concepts. Legal and illegal are not the same as right and wrong. Ethics is right for right's sake, while the law is a set of minimum standards that society will tolerate.

Political figures seem to be constantly defending their actions by pointing out they did nothing illegal. Escaping a criminal indictment does not make an act right. Most people expect those in positions of public trust not to meet just the minimum acceptable standards of the law, but to act in an ethical manner as well.

Just as some unethical acts can be legal, it is possible for illegal acts to be ethical. Laws on racial restrictions once were common. Some communities had laws prohibiting African-Americans from being inside city limits between sunset and sunrise. Segregation laws and some voting laws served unethical purposes. Violating these laws while they were upheld would have been illegal, but ethical, behavior.

Passing more laws will not end unethical behavior. While a law will deter some people, if a person wants to do something badly enough, he or she will find a way to do so regardless of any law.

Ethics and Motive

An act could be ethical or unethical depending upon the motive of the person performing the act. Assume that you used your best efforts to influence your state real estate licensing agency to tighten the requirements for real estate licensing by requiring greater education prior to licensing as well as more stringent examinations. If your action was based on your belief that this was necessary to provide the protection needed to the public, then your action would be ethical.

If the identical action was made for the self-serving purpose of keeping down the number of new competitors, then this action would be unethical, as it certainly would not pass the test of the Golden Rule.

Changing Ethics, Changing Laws

What is unethical but legal today might well be illegal in the future, because ethics precedes the law. In the 1970s, for example, a number of so-called "mortgage saviors" sought out homeowners who were in default on their home loans but had substantial equity in their homes. These "saviors" stopped the foreclosures by making the debtors' payments current. They often took second liens for the money they advanced. The terms of these liens were generally beyond the abilities of the debtors, so the "saviors" foreclosed and ended up owning the properties. In some instances, they took deeds from owners and gave the owners options to buy the homes back. Since the former owners were seldom able to exercise the options, the "saviors" took over the properties for the sole investment of making the foreclosing loan current.

Because of these "legal" abuses, California, for example, passed legislation during the 1980s making it illegal to take unconscionable advantage of owners in default. Behavior that was formerly unethical became illegal as well.

Excuses, Excuses, Excuses

Does a noble purpose justify the means used to achieve it? Some people will justify unethical conduct by claiming their duties to their families take precedence over their duties to others. This argument is really that the end does justify the means. Using such reasoning, one could justify any unethical act or crime if the end purpose was good. This reasoning rejects community in favor of self.

"If I didn't do it, someone else would" is an excuse often used. What the person is really saying is, "Someone will profit by unethical behavior so it is best that it be me." This reasoning also rejects the interests of others in favor of self.

For an ethical life, the worth of every human being should be regarded as morally important. People should be regarded as worth helping and not as tools or means to reach an end.

In order to show regard for others, we must be professionals, doing work in a skillful and helpful manner. Failure to serve the needs of others in a proper manner is failure to show regard for others. The real estate profession should lead, not follow, prevailing business morality. "Everybody does it" is an excuse heard all too often. We cannot accept unethical behavior in ourselves simply because others are doing the same thing.

Encouraging Ethical Excellence

If brokers fail to continually strive for improvement and to police themselves, consumer groups and the government will assume those responsibilities. The problem is that one unethical broker can reflect poorly on the entire real estate profession.

The National Association of REALTORS® has done a great deal to promote professionalism and to instill in licensees the concern that ethics must play a part in their daily lives. When a licensee joins a local board of REALTORS®, the licensee enters into an agreement to adhere to the rules of the organization. A violation of the rules is considered a violation against the local board, the members of the board and the National Association of REALTORS®.

Ideally, real estate practitioners should feel that they are part of a group and that they are mutually obligated to protect and promote the best interests of the public. They must be committed to real estate as a lifetime profession, not as a stopgap until they can find a more suitable vocation. Commitment fosters professionalism. As real estate agents, we meet one of the most basic needs of our community. The job is important and must not be taken lightly. It is not enough for us to talk an ethical course of action. We must live it ourselves and work so that others will also act in an ethical manner.

Codes of Ethics

The REALTORS® Code of Ethics was first adopted in 1913. The first paragraph of this code read as follows:

> "The real estate agent should be absolutely honest, truthful, faithful and efficient. He should bear in mind that he is an employee—that his client is his employer and is entitled to the best service the real estate man can give—his information, talent, time, services, loyalty, confidence and fidelity."

Note the use of the term *real estate man*. Today, more than half of the profession are women.

Other real estate professional organizations, among which is the National Association of Real Estate Brokers, Inc., have codes of ethics. These ethical codes indicate the sincere interest that all real estate professionals place on ethical excellence.

The present Code of Ethics and Standards of Practice of the National Association of REALTORS® (effective January 1, 1995) is reprinted in full in Appendix A. It is an excellent introduction to an understanding of ethical conduct within the real estate industry.

The National Association of REALTORS® has published *Interpretations of the Code of Ethics* to help REALTORS® and REALTOR-ASSOCIATE®S understand the ethical obligations created by the Code of Ethics, and as a reference work for grievance committees, ethics and arbitration hearing panels, and boards of directors. This manual utilizes cases to aid in the interpretation of the Code of Ethics.

The REALTOR® Code of Ethics is important to every real estate licensee regardless of whether he or she is a member of the National Association of REALTORS®. A careful reading will reveal that it is a pertinent guide to professional dealings with others. Adherence to the code will serve the best interests of buyers, sellers and the public in general, as well as help to enhance the professionalism of our industry. Many state regulatory agencies have used the REALTOR® code as a guideline for developing real estate regulations within their state. The REALTOR® code also is used frequently in courts to establish a guide to standards of care in real estate practice.

Several state licensing agencies have developed their own codes of ethics. In California, the Regulations of the Real Estate Commissioner include an Ethics and Professional Conduct Code. This example of a state code is included in Appendix B. The importance of ethics in real estate is an international concern. The National Association of Estate Agents, a British trade group, has prepared a detailed paper entitled "Ethics in Estate Agency," which is used as a training aid for member agents.

The Ideal

In our modern society it probably is not possible for an individual to live in an absolutely honest manner. A completely honest person, who refused to tell white lies to protect the feelings of others, likely would have few, if any, friends. White lies can create ethical dilemmas. As an example, assume the buyers of a new home you sold invite you in later to view their decorating efforts. You may feel the results reflect bad taste, and if asked your opinion, you might reply, "You have done a truly marvelous decorating job; I know this home will give you many years of enjoyment." In this case, your buyers wanted positive reinforcement, not necessarily the absolute truth.

Although the truly ethical life may be unachievable, you should still strive to achieve it. Thomas Watson, former president of IBM, stated, "If you reach for a star you will never get a star but neither will you get a handful of mud." He meant that we should strive for an ideal. Although we may never reach it, if we didn't have that ideal, we would never raise ourselves at all.

Case Study: When the "Letter of the Law" Is Unethical

Broker Wright, of Wright Realty, has one of the largest and oldest offices in town. He is active in civic affairs, gives generously to charities and is the past president of the local REALTOR® Association.

Pierce, a salesperson for Wright, lists the home of Mr. and Mrs. Caine under a three-month, exclusive right-to-sell agreement. Mr. Caine has recently been promoted, and the Caines have placed a reservation on a much larger home being built in Orchard Heights, a suburban subdivision. On February 4, one month after the Caine house is listed, Mr. Caine is seriously injured in a highway accident. On February 5, James Davis, a salesperson with Sandoval Realty, brings in a full-price offer on the Caine home from a prospect who had seen the house a week earlier.

The next day, broker Wright presents the offer, but Mrs. Caine says her husband will be confined to a wheelchair for the rest of his life and they could not possibly move into Orchard Heights. She mentions that the developer voluntarily returned their deposit that day, thereby releasing them from their contract. She also indicates that she had left a message on Pierce's answering machine explaining that a sale now would be out of the question. Broker Wright informs Mrs. Caine that if she does not accept the offer she will be obligated to pay the full commission, since his office had performed in accordance with the listing by finding a buyer who was ready, willing and able to buy. Mrs. Caine becomes upset and asks broker Wright to leave.

Despite his demands, the Caines refuse to pay Wright the commission. Broker Sandoval suggests that Wright try to negotiate a lesser sum, and that if he is unable to negotiate a settlement with the Caines, to forget it. Wright replies, "What's right is right—they signed a listing and we did our part. I don't want a dime less or a dime more than I have coming." Shortly thereafter, he brings suit against the Caines for the commission.

Ms. Fine, chair of the local REALTOR® Associations grievance committee, comes to see Wright about the lawsuit. Wright becomes very upset at the implication that this is an ethical matter. He makes the following statement:

> "I can assure you that I operate on the highest ethical level. In my more than 20 years in business, I have never been successfully sued because of my real estate activities.

"As a matter of fact, when I realized that we had an offer after Mr. Caine's accident, I immediately checked with my attorney, Charlotte Gaines. Charlotte told me that, while it may be tough on them, we were legally entitled to force the Caines to pay. She said that several cases on record directly supported her conclusion, and I agreed with her.

"Besides, it would not be practical, nor would it be good business, to give up what I am legally entitled to. I know of two cases in town where sellers changed their minds and refused to sell; in both cases, they had to pay.

"This is a simple matter of right and wrong and, legally, I am right. I am sorry for their predicament, but it wasn't any of my doing. I am an ethical businessperson. I resent even the thought that my conduct is unethical.

"Just because I am a real estate broker doesn't mean I should forget good business practice. To give away what I am entitled to would not be good business. I am not bound to any stronger rules of conduct than is any other good businessperson.

"Furthermore, I understand that the Caine matter was discussed at the last meeting, which I couldn't attend. I don't want people talking about my activities—it's no one's business but mine. I don't want the whole town talking about this, and I don't want it getting in the newspapers."

Analysis

As you can see in the preceding example, broker Wright doesn't really understand what ethics is all about. Ethics deals with what is right, measured by the application of the Golden Rule. Wright equates ethics with legalities, but they are not the same. Laws only set forth minimum standards of conduct, behavior beyond which society will not tolerate. It is not enough that an act stay within the limits of the law. Remember, laws do not control the conscience. Ethics precede the law; in fact, ethical ideas eventually become law as they gain support. Therefore, ethical conduct is usually above the legal minimum required. For example, some major corporations recently tried to excuse foreign corporate bribes by stating that they were legal in the country in which they were made. The public, however, reacted negatively to this excuse for improper behavior. In these instances, the firms learned that an important test of ethics is whether an action will stand the light of publicity. In broker Wright's case, he obviously didn't think his actions could stand up under the light of publicity, as he didn't want the whole town to know what he was doing. He knew his actions would result in a negative reaction toward him and his firm.

In our example, broker Wright talked about being practical, in order to avoid making an ethical consideration. Practical solutions are not necessarily the ethical course of action.

It is easy to deceive yourself into believing that what is practical is right and proper, but without an honest self-evaluation an ethical life is not possible. At all times we must be honest with ourselves and not let self-interest affect our judgment—self-deception must be avoided.

In the example, broker Wright is disturbed when he finds that as a member of the real estate profession, he is held to a higher standard of conduct than are members of other business groups. Because other groups have lower standards of conduct does not excuse broker Wright. If he claims to be a professional, he must live up to his responsibilities toward a professional standard of conduct. His standard of conduct should not be based on what others are doing. Any standard of conduct must be based on what is right. Unfortunately, many people never bother to apply the Golden Rule to their daily actions. They fail to consider that what they are doing could possibly be wrong. They even fail to follow IBM's one-word advice for business ethics, "Think!" In the case of broker Wright, it is doubtful that he ever asked himself whether he would want to be treated in the same manner as he was treating the Caines.

Ethics Questions

Suggested answers to the questions in this and subsequent chapters are set in italics.

1. In your area, many brokers and real estate salespersons drift in and out of the real estate profession as the economy changes. It is believed that the mobile nature of this work force is a contributing factor in many legal and ethical problems. Your state licensing agency has asked you to recommend solutions to this problem. What could you recommend?

   a. *Require licensees to complete certain educational courses prior to licensing. This would reduce short-term, in-and-out employment and the use of real estate as a stopgap job. It would also benefit the public, because licensees would be better prepared to meet the needs of others.*

      Licensing requirements should be relevant and reasonable. Unreasonable standards could keep otherwise qualified individuals from entering the profession.

   b. *Perhaps you believe that a state recovery fund is needed, that the existing fund is not adequate to reimburse members of the public who are injured by licensees or that the state needs more investigators to investigate complaints and protect the public. If so, you could recommend that license fees be increased to finance these projects and funds. Higher fees might also reduce the number of "gypsy" agents who move in and out of the profession.*

   c. *Mandate strict continuing-education requirements to reduce the number of licensees who are not truly dedicated to the profession as well as to provide better trained licensees. Continuing education requirements might include a mandatory number of hours in areas of specific concern to your state licensing agency, such as trust-fund handling, agency, ethics and fair housing.*

2. Disreputable practices that have served to undermine public confidence in the real estate profession often are perpetrated not by licensees, but by dealers selling their own properties. Unfortunately, the public does not always understand the difference. Your local

brokers' organization has asked you to make recommendations on how to deal with this problem. What possible recommendations could you make?

The problem with dealers is significant. They are bound only by the minimum requirements of the law, a situation often detrimental to the public's interest. To protect the public, you could recommend one or more of the following:

a. *If your state does not require seller disclosures, seek legislation requiring that disclosure statements be given to all buyers prior to purchase, by brokers and owners alike, setting forth in a standard format all important facts concerning the property. Disclosure statements should also be given to sellers where seller-financing is involved.*

b. *Recommend that trade associations sponsor an advertising campaign to educate the public about the advantage of dealing with members.*

c. *Actively work to expose illegal and unethical acts not just of other licensees, but of anyone engaging in real estate–related activities.*

3. Your local brokers' organization puts you in charge of a "broker of the year" awards program. You have a number of awards to make. What criteria could you use to judge ethical and professional success?

a. *Involvement in the local brokers' organization*
b. *Willingness to help others*
c. *Reputation among peers*
d. *Professional designations earned*
e. *Conduct of salespeople employed by the broker*
f. *Regard of the broker by both former principals and customers*
g. *Number and nature of professional complaints about the broker's conduct (if any)*
h. *Number of sales or amount of earnings (While not a measure of personal integrity, it would be an indication as to how he or she communicates with buyers and sellers.)*

4. In the case study featured in this chapter, what do you think broker Wright could have done to deal ethically with the Caines?

    a.   *Explain to the Caines what efforts had been expended on their behalf considering direct and indirect office expenses, as well as the time the salesperson and broker expended on their behalf. Then, ask the Caines what they feel would be a just settlement.*

    b.   *Suggest to the Caines that the problem be arbitrated by the local professional organization or that a mediator be used to help in the resolution of the problem.*

    c.   *Ask the Caines to reimburse the brokerage firm for direct advertising costs only.*

    d.   *Offer condolences, and release the Caines from the listing without cost.*

5. It has been said that "words without actions are the assassins of ideals." How does this apply to ethics in real estate?

    A verbal claim of ethical conduct is meaningless unless the person making that claim tries to lead an ethical business life. We must judge our actions by what is ethical, not just by what is legal. We must also strive to encourage others to act in an ethical manner. Without action in our daily lives, all the words praising doing what is right become meaningless.

2. Responsibilities to Your Principal

Loyalty + Communication = A Successful Agent-Client Relationship

---

Whose Agent Are You?

Real estate brokers operate primarily as agents who represent a principal. An agent has a fiduciary duty to his or her principal that includes loyalty, obedience, full disclosure, diligence, due care and the duty to account for all funds received. There is also a duty of confidentiality that continues even after the agency has terminated.

A real estate agent can operate traditionally, representing the seller; can represent the buyer; or be a dual agent, representing both buyer and seller.

Sellers' Agents

Traditionally, most real estate agents have represented the seller, receiving their agency authority by means of a formal right-to-sell agreement known as a listing. The firm that lists the property is known as the listing broker and other brokerage firms working with the listing broker are called selling agents and usually are subagents of the listing broker, although they could elect instead to represent the buyer.

Because the agent represents the seller in a traditional agency agreement, buyers should be cautioned against revealing information to the selling agent that they would not want the agent's principal to know.

Buyers' Agents

Buyer agency is a fast-growing concept within the real estate profession. The buyer agent has a fiduciary duty to the buyer, not the seller. The agent uses his or her knowledge and efforts to further those interests. A buyer can confide in the agent as to matters such as purpose of purchase, extenuating circumstances, financial limitations and negotiating strategy, knowing that the information will not be given to a seller.

Buyer agents agree to use their best efforts to locate a property that best meets the buyer's needs and will assist the buyer in making the purchase. Buyer agency allows for separate agency representation for sellers and buyers. The buyer-agency agreement customarily provides that the buyer shall pay a fee if a purchase is made. Generally, the buyer is relieved of the obligation to pay a fee if the buyer's agent receives a designated share of the listing agent's commission.

Dual Agents

A dual agency exists when one agent represents the buyer and the seller in a transaction. If an agent were a buyer's agent and the buyer wished to purchase a property listed for sale with his or her agent, then there would be a dual-agency situation. Whenever there is a dual-agency situation, both buyer and seller should be fully informed of and consent to the dual agency.

In a dual agency arrangement, the buyer and seller should agree that the agent is to be precluded from disclosing confidential information received from either party so as not to provide one party an advantage at the expense of the other party. For example, the agent could not tell the buyer that the seller would accept less, nor could he or she tell the seller that the buyer would pay more.

Even though an agent may intend to be a seller's agent, statements to a buyer such as, "I will get you the best deal possible," have led buyers to believe that a seller's agent represented them. Courts in many cases have determined that a seller's agent had agency duties to the buyer when the agent's words or actions led the buyer to believe that the agent was serving him or her.

Agency Disclosure

Most states require a formal written agency disclosure to both buyer and seller. Even in the absence of a mandated disclosure, as an agent you have an ethical duty to make certain that buyers and sellers fully understand your agency role. Misconceptions can lead, at best, to anger and, at worst, to lawsuits or criminal prosecution. To start out right, you could make a statement such as the following to a prospective buyer:

> "Mr. and Mrs. Johnson, I want to fully explain my duties as a real estate agent and my responsibilities to the owners of property and to you.
>
> "I am a seller's agent and I am paid by sellers for successfully completing sales of their property. As a seller's agent, I regard you as customers. I do not represent you in negotiations, nor will I act in any manner inconsistent with the interests of the owners I represent.
>
> "However, I have duties toward you as well. I must make honest and full disclosures. If I know of anything detrimental about the property or anything that would negatively affect your proposed use for a property, I will fully reveal it to you. I will not deceive you in any manner. I will make every effort to find you a home that best meets your needs. I will answer any questions you may have about an area, property, financing or closing in a complete and honest manner. I will point out benefits of particular properties.
>
> "If you wish to make an offer on a property, the final decision on price and terms must be yours. Please keep in mind that I represent the sellers. Don't reveal any information to me that you would not be comfortable providing to the seller. As an example, it wouldn't be fair to you for me to reveal to the seller that you were willing to increase an offer that you made. I have a duty to present any offer I receive to the owner. If I do not believe accepting a

particular offer is in the best interests of my principal, I will recommend that he or she reject the offer or make a counteroffer. If I believe an offer is fair, I will recommend its acceptance.

"Do you have any questions? Do you understand my role? Is this arrangement satisfactory to you?"

To make certain that there is no misunderstanding as to agency status and duties, a written agency declaration should be made and signed by buyers as well as sellers. They should, of course, be given a copy of the agency declaration.

The agency disclosure should be modified to meet any special state requirements. The disclosure also should be modified if you elect either to be a buyer's agent only or to act in a dual-agency capacity.

Accepting Listings

Most agency relationships start with a listing. A seller's agency normally starts with a right-to-sell listing in which an owner, who is the agent's principal, agrees to pay a commission if the agent is successful in locating a buyer who is ready, willing and financially able to purchase, and the agent in turn agrees to use his or her diligence and best efforts to sell the property within the period of the listing. In the case of an exclusive listing, the owner agrees that the named agent will be the owner's sole agent during the term of the listing.

Listings are signed by the agent and principal(s) at the time the relationship is established.

In buyer-agency listings, the agent agrees to use his or her best efforts to find a property that meets the buyer's needs. The buyer may be responsible for the agent's fee. The buyer-agency contract should be signed at the time the agency relationship is established.

In both types of listings, the agent agrees to serve his or her principal's best interests. Listing agreements create an agency between the principal and the broker and are the property of the broker.

If the listing salesperson leaves his or her broker, the broker retains the listing unless other arrangements have been made.

In this circumstance, the broker still must fulfill his or her duty toward the principal. It would be unethical as well as a violation of the agency if a broker failed to use diligence in handling the principal's needs.

In such a situation, the listing would be assigned to another salesperson to take over the departing salesperson's duties and responsibilities.

Duty of Diligence

The frequently expressed attitude, "never turn down a listing," is unethical. Being diligent can mean turning down listings. For example, if a broker lacks the expertise necessary to handle the sale of a specialized property or to locate such a property, he or she should not accept the listing, because it would be impossible for the broker to provide service in a diligent manner. Likewise, if the listing is in an area in which the broker does not market property, he or she would be acting in an unethical manner by accepting the listing. It doesn't make any difference whether an owner or buyer, knowing these facts, still wants to list with that broker—a broker must be able to distinguish between what is within and what is beyond his or her limitations. An exception might be a situation in which the broker works closely with someone who has the required expertise with full disclosure to the owner or buyer.

A broker may, of course, refer an owner or buyer to another broker. A broker can reject any listing, but once a listing is accepted the broker has a duty to use care, skill and diligence to fulfill with integrity his or her duties to the principal.

Lack of continued diligence throughout the term of the listing is, of course, also unethical. If the agent becomes unable to fulfill the requirements of the contract with the principal, the agent must inform the principal at once and give the reasons. Providing diligent service on a sale listing includes distributing the listing information, showing the listing to other licensees, notifying prospective buyers, advertising, instructing the owner on showing preparation, checking financing and so on. In other words, the broker must actively take positive steps aimed at consummating a sale. In a buyer-agency listing, the agent must diligently search for a property that best serves the interests of his or her buyer.

It could be unethical for a part-time broker, who has significant limitations on the time he or she can devote to real estate matters, to take a listing without disclosing this condition to the owner. If the broker would be limited in his or her efforts, the owner must be informed.

Spreading the Word

The broker's duty to disseminate seller-listing information is not limited to the listing office, but includes other brokers as well, if the listing agent is authorized to cooperate with other agents. This should be done as quickly as possible. It would be unethical for a listing broker to hold a listing for the maximum time allowed by a multiple listing service in the hope that his or her office will sell it rather than risk having to split a commission. It is in the principal's best interest for the broker to do everything feasible to help effect a sale as quickly as possible.

It would generally be unethical, and in many states is a violation of the law, to enter into an exclusive-listing arrangement knowing that another exclusive listing contract is in effect for the same property. Doing so could subject the owner to the possibility of having to pay two commissions.

This ethical issue is not unique to the United States. In Great Britain, where real estate agents accept instructions rather than take listings, the Rules of Conduct of the National Association of Estate Agents state the following:

> "Before accepting instructions a member shall ascertain whether the prospective client has given sole agency and/ or sole selling rights to another agent. No attempt shall be made to induce the breaking of a valid sole agency and/or sole selling rights contract. If a prospective client wishes to give instructions regardless of a sole agency and/or sole selling rights contract, the member shall not accept instructions before advising the vendor that he thereby lays himself open to a possible liability for payment of two commission claims."

Excluding Former Prospects

Upon taking an exclusive listing, the broker has an obligation to determine if any problems may arise as a result of any former listings of the property where another agent might be entitled to a commission if a sale is consummated to a particular buyer. The new broker has an obligation to exclude any such prospects to protect the owner from possibly paying two commissions.

Note: In many states the protection or safety clause in a listing, which protects the agent from the owner selling to a prospect after the expiration of the listing, is not enforceable after a subsequent exclusive right-to-sell listing is entered into. This protects the principal from being obligated to pay two commissions.

Open Listings

Some agents accept open-sale listings, which are nonexclusive listings where a number of agents can be working on the same property. The sale by one agent or by the owner terminates all other open listings. Open-sale listings generally reduce the likelihood of a sale, because many agents will work on open-listed properties only when they don't have suitable exclusively listed properties available to show prospective buyers. An agent knows that if another office or the owner sells the property, then he or she will receive no compensation regardless of the effort expended.

Although accepting an open-sale listing is not in itself unethical, it would be unethical if the agent led the owner to believe that the chances of sale were similar to those of an exclusive listing. Because open listings generally are not in an owner's best interests, agents would have an affirmative duty to warn an owner about the reduced likelihood of a sale. In order to best meet the needs of owners, the REALTORS® Code of Ethics encourages exclusive listings.

Buyer listings generally are exclusive listings but may be open listings. A buyer should realize that under an open listing, the agent really is not obligated to search diligently for a property.

In some areas of the country, open listings are fairly common in commercial property.

Termination by Principal

Because an agency agreement requires consent of the principal and agent to the agency, either party can terminate the agency agreement, or listing. If a principal wrongfully terminates an exclusive agency agreement, however, he or she could be held liable for damages.

Regardless of the justification for termination, the agent is precluded from representing himself or herself in an agency capacity once the principal has notified him or her of the termination of the listing.

Wrongful representation could subject a principal to damages based on ostensible agency. Refusal to accept an owner's termination of agency would be unethical as well as a breach of law.

Overpriced Listings

Accepting a vastly overpriced listing can create an ethical problem. A listing at a price significantly above a reasonable value would not be fair to the owner. Buyers may not want to see it and other agents probably will not want to show it. Such an overpriced listing materially reduces the probability of a sale. By taking an overpriced listing, an agent could have difficulty exercising the degree of diligence and effort he or she agreed to exercise.

Some agents have been known to "buy listings" by appealing to an owner's greed and suggesting that they can obtain an unrealistically high selling price. Taking an overpriced listing with the secret intention of persuading the owner to lower the price would be deceit and should not be tolerated. In short, it is unethical for a seller's agent to suggest a sales price that cannot be supported by a market evaluation.

Ascertaining Value

An agent has an ethical duty to ascertain a property's market value.

In obtaining listings, agents generally provide comparables. They may give the owner listed prices of other properties on the market. There is nothing wrong in doing this, as long as the prices actually paid for comparable properties also are given to the owner. Because listed prices in some markets are considerably higher than actual sale prices, providing only listed prices could give owners unreasonably high expectations.

Agents often provide information on unsold, expired listings. Failure to point out that the reason for unsold listings is usually related to price could be unethical. Pricing a listing based on unsold comparables could reasonably be expected to result in another unsold listing.

In presenting comparables, agents have a duty to adjust the sale price of properties to take into account the differences in amenities of the properties, condition of the properties, locational differences, terms of sale and so on. Failure to do so could be unethical, as an apparent reasonable list price could be distorted.

If no known comparable properties have been sold recently, or if the agent lacks the expertise to make an informed evaluation, he or she has a duty to suggest the professional help of a licensed or certified appraiser. It is important to note that, in any case, the licensee's evaluation of value is not an appraisal. An appraisal is a formal process conducted by a licensed or certified appraiser. It would be deceiving and therefore unethical for a real estate licensee to refer to the broker's estimate of value prepared by the licensee as an appraisal.

An agent who is uncertain about a property's value could do a disservice to his or her principal by listing the property at a price set by the principal unless the principal has knowledge of recent comparable sales in the area. If the price is too high, it is unlikely the property will sell; too low a price would allow others to take advantage of your principal.

If, after taking a listing, an agent receives information indicating that the price set is too high or too low, the agent has the duty to immediately inform the principal and suggest a price that better meets the principal's best interests.

Because a buyer's agent also has a duty to best serve the buyer's interest, the buyer's agent should not recommend a purchase price unless the value of the property has been ascertained. The agent's recommendations of a price to be offered should be made based on market conditions, special interests or considerations of the buyer, known seller motivation and, of course, the agent's estimation of value.

Protecting the Principal's Interests

A licensee has a duty to protect his or her principal's reputation and interests. The licensee's principal could be the seller in case of seller agency, the buyer in case of buyer agency and even both buyer and seller should a dual agency relationship exist. Therefore, the licensee should not release personal data concerning a principal to other persons in a transaction, or to the general public, without the concurrence of the principal. Gossiping about a principal's affairs or making detrimental remarks likewise could breach the fiduciary relationship and would be ethically questionable.

As an aid in avoiding breach of confidentiality, an agent could avoid discussions on personal matters with both buyers and sellers unless they have a bearing on the property sale or purchase.

Selling agents have a duty to qualify prospects and to know with whom they are dealing before giving out detailed data on a principal's property. A related duty is confidentiality—a licensee can neither use confidential information received from the principal for personal use, nor can he or she provide such information to others without the principal's consent. This duty persists even after the agency relationship is terminated. As an example, if a listing agent has confidential information about an owner's dire financial position, the agent cannot provide this information to a prospective buyer, even after the listing expires. Similarly, if a buyer's agent knows how much a buyer is prepared to pay for a particular type of property, the agent cannot reveal this information to a seller even after the agency expires.

A broker has a duty to obey the lawful directions of the principal. This does not mean, however, that the principal can dictate such matters as the amount of advertising dollars to be spent or the conduct of the office. A broker who is unwilling to obey the lawful instruction of his or her principal should agree to a termination of the agency.

As an agent, the broker owes his or her principal the duty to exercise reasonable care. Thus, a listing broker should protect the owner's property. For example, a broker should not allow a prospective buyer to have a key in order to visit the property unescorted. A licensee is liable, of course, for any loss caused by his or her own negligence. For example, if the agent were managing the property, failure to maintain adequate insurance could be negligence. It could also be unethical for a broker who is a property manager to fail to take emergency measures to protect a property, if such measures were required, regardless of whether a broker had the specific authority to do so.

A licensee is expected to be familiar with laws or ordinances that affect the principal's property. Failure of the licensee to keep fully informed of such matters in areas where the licensee is working could be unethical, because the licensee would be failing to provide service in a diligent and professional manner.

Although selling agents must be honest with purchasers, complete honesty does not require revealing your principal's position. In fact, doing so would be a breach of agency, a violation of your duties to your principal. Nevertheless, deceit by an agent cannot be tolerated, even when the purpose of the deceit is to enhance the position of the agent's principal. For example, if a seller's agent knows that a price is not firm, telling a prospective buyer that the property cannot be purchased at less than the listed price would be false, and could work to the detriment of the prospective buyer. If a prospective buyer asks a seller's agent if the property could be purchased at a lower price, a proper reply could be, "Don't you think [$ (the list price)] is a reasonable price for the property?"

Should the prospective buyers indicate that they don't think the price is reasonable or simply that the price is more than they will pay, a proper response could be, "What would you be willing to pay for this property?"

If you receive a dollar figure, your response could be, "How did you arrive at [$]?"

The last comment has the prospective buyers justifying a price. It should tend to make the buyers more conducive to raising their estimate of value. A further statement could be, "I don't know if the owners will accept [$], but we can try. As you really like this home, why don't you raise the offer by just [5 percent] to [$]? I think it will increase your chances of ownership."

The duty of the seller's agent is to meet the best interests of the seller, which includes obtaining the most advantageous purchase offer possible. Rushing to write up any offer without attempting to maximize the offer would not be in your principal's best interest. Before you write up an offer for less than the listed price, explain that the greater the difference between the offer and the listed price and/or terms, the less the chance that the offer will be accepted.

Suggesting to a prospective buyer that the property could be purchased for less than the listed price or that he or she should offer less than the listed price would be, in most instances, a breach of fiduciary duty.

Without the permission of your principal, it would be a breach of agency duty to reveal any information to others that could work to the detriment of your principal. This could include the reason for the sale. If your principal was highly motivated to sell and the buyer knew it, a lower price might be offered and a competitive advantage in the negotiations might be lost. Similarly, knowing the details of another offer accepted or counteroffer given could give buyers an advantage that would not be in your principal's best interests.

As a buyer's agent, your duties are to the buyer's interests, which ordinarily are to obtain the property at the lowest price and/or best terms possible. In this regard you should relay to the buyer any pertinent information you have that might affect a seller's position and make recommendations for an offer that will best serve your principal's interest.

As a buyer's agent, you should not be concerned with obtaining a reduced price if the reduced price offer could work against your principal's best interests. A full price or even above full price offer could ethically be recommended where there are likely to be competitive offers or the buyer cannot afford to take the chance of not obtaining a particular property. The buyer should fully understand your reasoning as to your recommendations for any offer.

As a buyer's agent, you would not want to reveal any information to the seller that might weaken your buyer's bargaining ability, such as his or her need for a particular property or how much your buyer had previously paid for similar property.

Duty of Full Disclosure

Agents have a duty of full disclosure to the principal; they must give any known information that would affect the property and would reasonably be expected to be of interest to the principal. This would include the sale of similar property at a higher or lower price than offered by the principal, changes or planned changes in zoning within the area, planned development or redevelopment and so on.

If an agent makes any secret profit or is placed in the position of possibly receiving a secret profit, the agent has a duty of full disclosure. As an example, if a buyer informs a seller's agent that he or she will list his or her present home with the agent if the seller accepts the buyer's offer, this would have to be communicated to the seller. Urging acceptance of such an offer without disclosure could be considered self-dealing and a secret profit, a violation of licensing laws in most states.

Secret profits must be disclosed, regardless of whether the owner is treated fairly. As an example, a property manager who buys supplies wholesale and adds a handling charge when billing to owners must reveal and obtain owners' agreements as to that charge even though the prices paid by owners are less than they would pay if they purchased the supplies themselves.

If a seller's agent knows the buyer has borrowed or will borrow the down payment, the principal should be told of the loan, especially if the principal will retain any interest in the property or finance the buyer in any manner. A buyer's borrowing the down payment is important to a principal because it increases the chances that the buyer will default on the payments. The fact that the buyer will borrow the down payment also will have an impact on the buyer's ability to obtain the necessary financing.

The seller's agent has a duty to make certain that the sellers fully understand what the closing costs will be and what will actually be netted from a sale prior to their acceptance of any offer. The agent obtaining an offer must make certain that the buyers understand closing costs and what their financial commitment will be as to closing requirements and likely payments.

If the acceptance of an offer would result in the principal's having to put up cash to close the transaction because of liens, loan and title costs or seller points, the seller's agent has an affirmative duty to inform the principal of this fact. Allowing a principal to accept an offer without fully understanding the consequences of acceptance could be regarded as unethical conduct.

In a recent court case, a principal sold a home through a broker. Instead of carrying back a mortgage on the property sold, the principal took a mortgage on raw land that the buyer owned. The buyer defaulted and the security for the mortgage proved to be inadequate. In that state it was not possible to obtain a deficiency judgment in the case of seller financing, so the principal suffered a loss. The court held that the broker was liable to the principal for the loss. The broker was held to have had a duty to investigate the adequacy of the consideration and to explain the dangers of carrying back a mortgage on another property. The broker had a positive duty to protect the best interests of the principal and failed to do so.

In several states, a number of purchasers bought homes with no down payment. They agreed to assume existing loans and pay off the sellers' equity in full within a short period, such as 60 days. The reasons generally given were that they were selling another property and would not have the money until then, but needed a home immediately. A number of brokers handled these types of sales as seller's agents. The buyers immediately rented the homes, and made no payments on the loans assumed, resulting in foreclosure. In many cases they were able to collect rent for a year or more before their interests were foreclosed. One purchaser purchased several hundred properties in this manner. Although the agents had no participation in the purchaser's fraud, they probably were guilty of unethical conduct because they failed to recommend adequate safeguards for their sellers. By failing to recommend that the closings be delayed until the money was paid and by not suggesting legal advice, they made the fraud possible. This practice of "equity skimming" resulted in the passage of laws that have substantially eliminated this practice. Licensees should, however, be alert to any situation where a buyer is to gain control of property prior to meeting his or her purchase commitments.

Avoiding Conflicts of Interest

A licensee has a duty to represent the principal faithfully. It could be unethical to list a property for sale if your office or a firm related to yours is in the business of buying and selling property of the same type as a principal. For example, if your office buys, operates and sells apartment buildings as a principal, you generally should not list such buildings for sale. If a broker takes a listing under these circumstances, he or she in effect could be competing with the owner for buyers. Like most humans, a broker might place self-interest above the interests of the principal in such a situation, thus breaching agency duties. The agent has a duty not to compete with the principal; the agent must not become an adversary to the principal. A person can be either a principal or an agent in a given situation, but conflicts of interest occur when one tries to do both. Even if no actual conflict of interest exists, an agent should avoid even the appearance of a conflict of interest. Such an appearance reflects negatively on the entire real estate profession.

A licensee should not take a listing if, at the time of the listing, the agent knows that a party unknown to the owner will be making an offer on the property. A licensee should not inject himself or herself into a listing situation where an offer is expected to take place without the agent's intervention. It would, however, be proper to take the listing if the agent discloses the likely offer as well as the benefits the agency could provide. As an alternative, the agent could ethically take the listing with the exclusion of the named buyer or offer to assist with the transaction at a reduced commission.

Some companies will not allow their salespeople to purchase office listings for resale. Other offices will allow their salespeople to purchase an office listing only after it has been exposed to the market for a stated period. Some offices will not even allow their salespeople to purchase listings for resale that are listed by other offices if their office shares in the commission as a subagent of the listing broker. The reason for this is to avoid the appearance of a conflict of interest when an agent representing a seller purchases a property for resale. If the agent believes the property is underpriced, then the agent had a duty to tell the owner. If the agent thinks he or she knows of or can locate a buyer at a higher price, the agent has a duty to disclose this to the owner as well. If the agent believes a few thousand dollars in cosmetic work will materially increase the value, the owner is entitled to the benefit of the agent's expert advice.

Even with full disclosure, many brokers feel that a rapid resale at a significantly higher price may give the appearance of unethical self-dealing, this reflects negatively on the firm and the entire real estate profession. If an agent is to be a dealer, one way to avoid an actual conflict of interest or the perception of one is to deal entirely as a principal, with neither the agent nor his or her broker sharing in any portion of commission.

A serious conflict of interest could exist if a buyer's agent also buys and sells property as a principal. The buyer's agent has a conflict of interest and has breached fiduciary duty if he or she purchases a property of a type being sought by one of his or her clients without first offering the property to that client.

The agent has a duty of full disclosure if property owned by an agent, the agent's family members or others with whom the agent has a close personal or business relationship is offered to that agent's buyer. While the sale would not be improper if full disclosure were made, failing to disclose such an interest or relationship would at the very least raise a question as to conflict of interest. In many states, buyers' and sellers' agents have these disclosure duties imposed by law.

Article 4 of the REALTORS® Code of Ethics states:

> "REALTORS® shall not acquire an interest in or buy or present offers from themselves, any member of their immediate families, their firms or any member thereof, or any entities in which they have any ownership interest, any real property without making their true position known to the owner or the owner's agent. In selling property they own, or in which they have any interest, REALTORS® shall reveal their ownership or interest in writing to the purchaser or the purchaser's representative."

Disclosure alone probably would not be adequate when a buyer's agent sells his or her own property to a principal. Application of the Golden Rule would make it appear improper for the buyer to buy from the agent and also have to pay the agent a fee for finding the agent's own property. The agent should relieve the buyer of paying a fee when the buyer purchases a property owned by the buyer's agent.

Agents' Fees

Several states require that before an agreement of sale is entered into, the broker must present the seller with a written statement of estimated costs, such as broker's commissions, points, prepayment penalties, title insurance or abstract charges, escrow fees, existing encumbrances to be paid and so on, including the net balance the seller will receive. When a licensee represents the seller, the licensee has a duty to give the seller such an estimate both at the time of listing and when presenting an offer for acceptance. Sellers frequently do not understand the concept of points. If, for example, discount points are to be paid by the seller for a buyer's loan, the licensee must make sure that the seller fully understands this obligation and that it is clearly set forth in the purchase contract.

If a broker takes an advance-fee listing (a fee given to a broker to cover advertising costs, usually in a magazine or brochure distributed by the broker), he or she must disclose to the principal how the fee is to be used and the reasonable value of the services given. Failure to do so could be unethical conduct. There are some advance-fee brokers that charge such a high fee that they make a major portion of their profit from the difference between the advanced fee charged and their actual costs.

Adjustable Fees

Should an agent charge the same fee for a property that the agent knows will readily sell as for a property that is expected to be fairly difficult to sell? Some critics claim that fees unrelated to difficulty of performance are unethical because they penalize owners with highly salable property and benefit those who are selling less desirable property. Some brokers have experimented with sliding fee scales, but this solution has led to greater problems. Because fees based on difficulty of sale are highly subjective, owners subject to fees higher than others tend to feel they are being treated unfairly.

When sales are likely to be made through cooperative brokerage, agreeing to a fee that would result in a cooperating broker receiving a fee that would not be acceptable to you, if you were the selling agent, could be unethical unless the possible effects of such a fee were explained to and approved by the owner. An unacceptable fee might be detrimental to your principal because it could serve as a disincentive to show the property if other similar property offered more acceptable fees to the selling agent.

Some agents who charge more competitive fees take the cut themselves in cobrokerage situations. As an example, assume a broker charges a 5 percent fee when the majority of brokers charge 6 percent and usually split the commission with the selling office. If the broker who charges 5 percent provides 3 percent to successful cooperating selling brokers, and the lower fee does not affect the listing broker's advertising or diligence in pursuing a sale, then the disclosure would not be necessary, except possibly as an incentive to obtain the listing.

If an owner has to sell quickly, an agent probably would have a duty to explain the benefits of agreeing to a greater fee than was usual or a below-market price, or both. This could result in greater interest by other agents and could increase the likelihood of a quick sale.

Unethical Fees

Breaches of ethics can take many forms, including fees and fee structures. Some unethical fees follow:

- A net listing (one in which the broker gets all monies beyond a set amount of the sales price) is inherently unethical and, in many states, is illegal. If a broker takes a net listing, he or she in effect speculates with the client's property. Asking a greater amount than that for which the property is listed is not in the client's best interests, because it could inhibit attempts at a speedy sale. In addition, net listings allow too much possibility for fraud, which cannot be condoned.
- A listing combined with an option whereby the broker can buy the property at an agreed price is also unethical. Under the listing, the licensee would be entitled to a commission, but by having an option, the licensee in effect has a net listing. The broker's interest in this situation would not be compatible with that of the principal.

- Kickbacks, or rebates, must be regarded as secret profit. It is unethical for an agent to accept kickbacks of cash, gifts or favored treatment on his or her own transactions for suggesting attorneys, title insurers, home protection plans, escrows, lenders, termite companies and so on, unless all parties to the transaction are fully aware of the kickbacks and agree to them. In many states, kickbacks are illegal regardless of disclosure.

Avoiding Fraud and Unethical Acts

The National Association of Estate Agents, the British trade group of real estate agents, considers solicitation of bereaved inheritors to be unethical conduct. The authors do not believe that contacting heirs is, in and of itself, unethical. If, however, the surviving heirs were in an emotional frame of mind shortly after the death of a close family member, continuing such solicitation could be unethical. Of course, it would be unethical to indicate an exaggerated or nonexistent relationship with the deceased to increase the likelihood of obtaining a listing.

Any listing that authorizes a licensee to execute the sales agreement by utilizing a power of attorney would be uncalled for in all but the most unusual circumstances. An agreement such as this could work to the detriment of the principal, who could be forced to sell at the listed price even if conditions changed. Likewise, provisions that authorize the broker to confess judgment against the principal if an earned commission is not paid should be avoided. (A confession of judgment allows the broker to record a judgment against the principal without any legal proceedings.) It is considered illegal in several states, because such a provision deprives the principal of his or her day in court.

A broker should not be a party to any form of fraud. If a broker were asked to postdate a sale or indicate a false price for IRS reporting, he or she must refuse to do so.

For example, a Florida broker arranged a number of sales where buyers used cash for purchases, but the purchase contracts provided for the purchase price to be paid privately outside of escrow. The broker's action made it possible for buyers to convert drug money to real estate without having the cash deposited in a trust account, which would have required federal disclosure. The broker's actions were, of course, unethical. In this case, the broker was held criminally liable for his involvement in an illegal money-laundering scheme.

If you give legal advice regarding the tax consequences of a sale, your actions could be construed as the unauthorized practice of law, unless, of course, you are also a practicing attorney. Suggesting ways to avoid taxes, such as assuring a party that no one will check, would not only be unethical but could be considered a conspiracy to defraud the government.

When an offer is received, the broker has an ethical and legal duty to ensure that the entire agreement is reduced to writing, and not left to oral understandings. If an offer requires that everything be in "good and proper condition," the licensee should point out to the owner that this could create unexpected liabilities for unknown latent defects. The licensee could suggest a counteroffer that spells out exactly what is warranted or allows the buyer to inspect and accept the property at a particular date. If an offer requires the principal to finance part of the purchase price, the licensee should obtain information on the buyer's employment and ability to pay, as well as a credit report on the buyer.

As previously stated, if a buyer is related to the licensee by blood, marriage or business or other close/personal association, this fact must be made known to the sellers prior to their acceptance. In this situation, a licensee must not make a secret profit or allow a situation to develop in which there was even an appearance of impropriety. This reflects on the broker's reputation as well as on that of the entire real estate profession.

Listings frequently include safety clauses that entitle the broker to a commission for sales made after the listing expires when the broker registers his or her prospects prior to the expiration of the listing and a registered prospect buys during the safety period. It could be unethical for a broker to register prospects with an owner when he or she had only mentioned the property without actually showing them the property or attempting to obtain offers from them. Since the broker has not diligently pursued the prospects, he or she should not be entitled to any commission for listing their names.

The broker must use diligence until the property is sold and closed or the listing expires. The broker should not stop advertising, remove signs or tell others the property is sold until an offer has been accepted.

Many firm offices have a policy of allowing owners to decide whether the property should continue to be shown after an offer has been accepted. Should another buyer wish to make an offer, it would be in your principal's best interest to take the offer as a backup. The offeror would have to be fully informed of the backup nature of the offer and, of course, the offer would have to be promptly presented to the owner as a backup offer.

When a sale is closed and the agency relationship is over, a broker is no longer an agent and thus cannot represent himself or herself to be one. However, the agent should remember that the agency duty of confidentiality continues indefinitely.

Case Study: When the Agent's Interest Is Not the Principal's Best Interest

Darlene Donahue is the broker for Fast-Sell Realty. When a "For Sale by Owner" sign went up in her neighborhood, broker Donahue called on the owners, Mr. and Mrs. Patel, and said, "I am interested in your home. May I come by to see it?" After viewing the home, she asks the owners what they wanted for their home. Mr. Patel replied, "$100,000." Broker Donahue then told him, "I am the broker with Fast-Sell Realty and I can help you." She convinced the owners to give her a listing, which she takes for $110,000. Broker Donahue said, "It will give us some room to negotiate." Broker Donahue wrote the listing with an 8 percent commission. Mr. Patel said, "I suppose 8 percent is pretty standard." Broker Darlene did not reply, but instead asked the owners additional questions about the property.

At the sales meeting the next day, broker Donahue tells her salespeople about her "great" listing. She points out that the property shows well, has terrific landscaping and would normally be expected to sell for between $140,000 and $150,000. She repeats to her salespeople several times that this is an 8 percent deal. (All other residential listings the firm had are at 6 percent.) She tells one of her salespersons, "I particularly want you to call that dealer you have worked with, Magda Garcia; it's the sort of bargain she should go for, and she always relists her purchases with our firm."

Analysis

Even before the agency began, broker Donahue entered the Patels' home under subterfuge. While she did not specifically state she was a buyer, the Patels would have been reasonable in making this assumption from broker Donahue's statement, "I am interested in your home. May I come by to see it?" Her words clearly were intended to hide from the Patels the fact that she was a broker. Because deceit such as this does not pass the test of the Golden Rule, it must be regarded as unethical conduct.

By raising the Patels' asking price $10,000 with the statement, "It will give us some room to negotiate," it could reasonably be interpreted by the Patels to mean that their $100,000 price was a fair market price. This really compounds broker Donahue's unethical behavior. She failed to serve her principals' best interests by failing to inform them that the price they were asking was significantly below what their home could reasonably be expected to sell for. While a below-market listing could be in the best interests of the owners in situations where an immediate sale is necessary, those facts were not indicated in this case. By taking a below-market listing, broker Donahue increased the likelihood of a sale and a commission at the expense of the owners.

When Mr. Patel said, "I suppose 8 percent is pretty standard," he was really asking a question. Broker Donahue should have answered it, but instead chose to avoid giving any answer by changing the subject. Mr. Patel could reasonably assume from the lack of response that his supposition was correct.

While commissions should be negotiable, taking advantage of an uninformed seller raises an ethical question. If broker Donahue had her auto repaired and paid a higher price for the work because of her lack of mechanical knowledge, she would be outraged should she learn of the true facts. This situation is analogous to the Patels' lack of knowledge as to commission structure in the area as applied to residential property. There could be situations such as low dollar sales as well as sales requiring greater-than-normal broker effort that would warrant a higher commission. From broker Donahue's repetition of "8 percent," it is clear that broker Donahue did not think a higher commission was warranted by the property and that 8 percent was an unusually high commission.

In suggesting that a salesperson call Magda Garcia, broker Donahue was hoping to turn the one sale into two sales and two commissions, which could mean a secret profit. This would work to the benefit of Fast-Sell Realty at the expense of the Patels. Again, broker Donahue's actions fail to pass the test of the Golden Rule.

The Patels could file a complaint to the state licensing agency about broker Donahue's actions as well as file a grievance with the local professional real estate organization, if broker Donahue is a member. The Patels could cancel their listing or, if a sale was made, bring legal action against broker Donahue for damages.

Ethics Questions

1. At noon, you receive a full-price offer from Allied Realty on a property you have listed. You immediately call the owners and make an appointment to meet with them at 7:00 that night. At 4 P.M., you receive another full-price offer from Sterling Realty, and at 5:30 P.M. your salesperson, Sue San Marco, calls to say she has a customer coming in from out of town who had previously seen the property and would be presenting an offer at 8 A.M. the next day. When you arrive at the owner's home at 7 P.M., what do you tell them ? What course of action could you suggest?

   You should present both offers and tell your principals about the offer expected the next day. You could obtain the owner's permission to tell all three prospective buyers that there are competing offers for the property and invite them to come up with new offers, with the property to be sold to the highest bidder.

   You should point out, however, that this course of action is dangerous, for the following reasons:

   - *Most buyers don't want to become involved in a bidding war.*
   - *Asking for new offers is a rejection of the offers received.*
   - *If you suggest a counteroffer to one, you would not be really fair to the others.*

   In short, by negotiating for a higher bid at this point, all three buyers could be lost. An acceptance, on the other hand, would form a binding contract.

   You also should evaluate all terms of the offers, as full-price offers are not necessarily equal, considering financing, contingencies, closing time and so on. Before an offer is accepted, especially where there are competing offers, the credit-worthiness of the buyer should be ascertained. Otherwise, the owner could accept an offer from an unqualified buyer while rejecting an offer from a qualified buyer.

2. After the acceptance of an offer on the Iqbal's property, you receive a call from Mr. Sark, who had previously seen it. You tell Mr. Sark that an offer has been accepted. He asks what it sold for, and you tell him the price was $92,000. Mr. Sark is surprised that the property sold at that low a price, because it had been listed at $110,000. One

hour later, Mr. Sark is in your office with an offer for $97,000. You inform him that you cannot accept the offer, but he threatens to sue if you don't present it. You tell the Iqbals that they cannot accept the offer, but Mr. Iqbal calls Mr. Sark and asks how soon they could close if he accepted. Mr. Sark replies that he can close within a week. The Iqbals then accept Sark's offer. After the sale, the Iqbals move to Mexico, where they plan to retire. The first buyer, Ms. Samuels, calls to ask why someone else is moving into her new home. When you tell her what happened, she becomes angry with you. Does she have cause? What could you do to protect yourself in the future?

Unless the Iqbals had specifically authorized you to disclose the selling price, you should not have; this information is confidential, and Mr. Sark had no legitimate need to know it. You were right in taking the Sark offer, because you have a duty to present all offers, even after another has been accepted. These can be backup offers in case the first buyer defaults.

You were correct in advising against acceptance of Sark's offer after the previous offer has been accepted; to do otherwise would have been inducing a breach of contract. Some brokers suggest that owners sign a statement to the effect that, after an offer is accepted, the broker is not to take or present any subsequent offers. This might relieve the broker of the problem in a case such as this. In some states, though, any failure to present an offer would violate state statutes. In this example, Mr. Sark might be held liable in tort for interfering with an advantageous contract and inducing the Iqbals to breach it.

When the Iqbals accepted Mr. Sark's offer, you also breached your duty to inform Ms. Samuels of this detrimental fact. (For more information on the broker's duty to the buyer, see Chapter 3.)

3. A former client, Ms. Anderson, calls you to say she wishes to list her farm for sale with you. When you arrive, she states, "I think the farm should bring $440,000, and that's what we should list it for." You feel that this is an excellent buy, and you tell Ms. Anderson that you have been interested in obtaining a farm. Instead of taking a listing, you buy the farm for $440,000. Three months later, you resell the farm for $560,000. Have you made an honest profit?

Called in as an agent, you changed your status to that of a principal. Even though an agency agreement was not signed, Ms.

Anderson had asked you to represent her. She expected agency duties and as an agent you had a duty to tell Ms. Anderson what you thought the farm should sell for. You also said you wanted a farm, which was not the whole truth. What you wanted was a profit. Your actions in this case would be unethical.

4. You receive an offer on property that you have listed. The offer is in accordance with the listing, requiring 20 percent down and the balance over the next five years, but the price is 15 percent below the listing. You have heard rumors that the buyer, Allied Investment, has been having financial difficulties; however, you do not mention this to the owner, because you think gossiping is unethical. The owner agrees to accept the offer only if you reduce your commission from 5 percent to 4 percent, which you agree to do. After the sale, you receive and accept from the buyer a case of imported champagne for your efforts. What are the ethical problems in this situation?

   You had a duty to tell the owner about the rumors regarding Allied Investment, because the owner will be financing the buyer. You should have suggested a complete credit report to verify or remove any doubt about the buyer's financial condition. There is nothing unethical in reducing a commission when the price is reduced; however, the gift of champagne, though not requested, amounts to a secret profit. You should ask the owner's permission for you to accept the gift. If denied, you should return it.

5. You receive a $440,000 offer with 15 percent down on a property listed at $490,000 with 30 percent down. In order to persuade the seller to accept, you request a financial statement from the buyer, which is supplied. With the aid of this statement you get the owner to accept. Within a year, the buyer defaults. This financial statement was a sham, with vastly overrated values. Was your course of action ethical?

   Because you requested the financial statement as a means of persuading the owner to accept, you had a duty either to ascertain if the statement was factual or to recommend that the seller have an accountant review the buyer's financial capabilities. Your failure to do so was negligent and, therefore, questionable conduct.

Because the seller was to be carrying 85 percent of the sale price, you should also have recommended that the seller seek legal counsel.

6. You list an apartment building for $207,000. You order an appraisal from a mortgage company regarding the amount they will loan on the property. You tell the owner that if he "fudges" a little on the income and "hedges" on expenses, the appraisal will be more advantageous to him. You advertise the property as "asking $207,000." You receive an offer from a racially mixed couple. When you present the offer, you don't mention the buyers' races, even though your principal intends to remain in the building as a tenant. The owner, who is obviously intoxicated when you arrive, says, "You sold this damn place! Good! Where do I sign?" even though he had not yet heard the terms of the offer. Since you consider the offer fair, you have the owner sign. What are the ethical problems here?

    Your advice to the owner was unethical. You suggested that he provide false data with fraudulent intent. This amounts to fraud upon the lender. By advertising, "asking $207,000," you indicated the owner would accept less. In many areas of the country, the word asking *implies that a price is not firm. This is unethical to do without the owner's permission.*

    You were right in not telling the owner that the buyers were a racially mixed couple, because this should have no bearing on the sale. But you should not have allowed the owner to accept the offer while intoxicated, because he obviously was ready to accept anything. The owner must fully understand the terms of the offer prior to signing.

7. In reviewing your records, you find that in the four months during which you have had a listing on the Henry farm, you have placed more than 60 ads but have not had a single showing. You decide to discontinue advertising for the remaining two months of the listing. Is your action ethical?

    By canceling the ads without the owner's knowledge or consent, you have breached your promise to use your diligence and best efforts to obtain a buyer. You have given up on marketing the farm. This is a breach of your promise to use diligence, as well as unethical conduct. You could have suggested to the owner a mutual recision of the listing, or an alternative approach to marketing the property if feasible.

8. You obtain a full-price offer of $340,000 on a large warehouse that you have listed. The buyer's attorney inserts a clause in the offer: "Seller warrants that all plumbing and mechanical equipment are in good and proper working order." When you present the offer, the seller asks you to explain this clause. You tell her it means that everything works, such as overhead doors, elevators and so on. The owner signs and three months later she calls you, saying that the new buyers intend to sue. The sprinkler system, which met the local codes when installed, does not meet present codes. The fire insurance carrier says it will cancel unless the system is brought up to present codes. The low bid for this work is $120,000. Is this your problem?

   You erroneously explained a clause that could have far-reaching effects. Equipment "in good and proper working order" could be interpreted to mean that the equipment meets local and state codes. You could be held liable if the seller has to reimburse the buyer. You could have suggested to the seller that a counteroffer be made, either specifying what was warranted or giving the buyer an opportunity prior to closing to inspect the property and either reject or accept it.

   You should not have given your legal interpretation of the clause. Instead, you should have recommended that the owner seek legal advice.

9. You receive two cash offers for a property through two of your salespeople. One offer is for $127,000 and includes a $3,500 cashier's check as earnest money. The other offer is for the list price of $130,000 and includes a $2,000 check as earnest money. You present both offers, and the higher one is accepted. The $3,500 is returned to the other party. Several days later the $2,000 check bounces because of insufficient funds. You check the buyer's resources, and it is apparent that he doesn't have the ability to raise the cash nor does he have the income to be able to obtain financing for the property. You contact the other buyers, but it takes two days to reach them. They inform you that they have purchased another property. You sadly call the owners to tell them the bad news. The owners claim you blew it. What did you do wrong?

You failed to act in the best interests of the owner. It is not unusual for a sale to fail to close because of financial problems. In a situation such as this, with two similar offers, prudence would dictate that you make a reasonable effort to determine the financial abilities of the offerors.

Since both offers were from your own salespeople, you could have checked the extent that the salespersons had financially qualified the buyers. You could have also requested offerors to supply you with a copy of their credit reports or financial statements.

Your apparent failure to consider financial difficulties when there were competing offers was at best unprofessional. Your failure to immediately inform the owners of the bounced check allowed the owners to continue in their belief that their house was sold. It could have resulted in the owners making a commitment based on this belief. Application of the Golden Rule as to your failure to immediately convey bad news would indicate a breach of ethics.

10. Lillian Swenson, a buyer's broker, overheard a conversation between a listing broker and another agent at a board meeting. She learned that builder Levitsky was desperate for cash. While he was asking $180,000 for a new home he had built, Levitsky only had $130,000 in the home because he had purchased the lot at a bargain price. Broker Swenson contacts one of her clients, Markus Jefferson, who places an offer of $124,000 for the home with no contingencies and closing within 20 days. The offer was based on broker Swenson's recommendation. The owner accepts. Was broker Swenson operating in an ethical manner?

As a buyer's agent, broker Swenson's duty was to the buyer. She had a duty to best serve the interests of that buyer. While the offer she formulated may have given her client a bargain, it also met the seller's immediate needs or the offer wouldn't have been accepted. It is ethical to use whatever knowledge you have to assist your client, providing the knowledge was not obtained by illegal means or is a breach of a confidence.

If broker Swenson had purchased the home herself to personally take advantage of a bargain, then she would have breached an agency duty as she was a buyer's broker. Not offering a client a home that met his or her needs because the agent would make more acting as a principal is unethical conduct and breaches agency duty.

The listing agent who divulged the information breached agency duties if the disclosure was made without owner approval. Obviously, the listing agent was looking for an easy sale by letting others know that a real bargain was possible.

11. Mr. Smith, who has previously purchased and sold property through your firm, comes to your office and says he wants to sell two lots in the Sunnyside subdivision. This is a nice subdivision on the other side of town, where you seldom have listings. Mr. Smith says he paid $4,900 each for the lots seven years earlier, and asks you what he could get for them now. You recall that your firm had sold a lot in this subdivision, and, upon checking, you discover that two years earlier you had listed that lot for $9,800, and it has taken six months to sell. It sold to a builder for $8,600 cash. You inform Mr. Smith that since real estate prices had been increasing you think you should list the lots at $11,900 each, which, while the price might be a little high, would be a good price to start with. Mr. Smith agrees. After obtaining this listing, you call Hank Green, the builder who had purchased that other lot for $8,600. You tell him about the listing. Mr. Green says he will take both lots, and 20 minutes later he is at your office and signs full-price offers. Before you can get the offer accepted, a friend, broker Stout, comes to your office to return a key. You tell him of your one-hour listing and sale. Broker Stout says he wished he had known about the listings because he would have purchased them himself. He tells you he has handled two recent sales in the subdivision, one for $18,900 and one for $21,000. For some reason, he says, the sales have taken off in the subdivision during the past year and the few remaining vacant lots have really gone up in value. At this point, has there been any unethical action on your part? What should you do now?

    You should not have set a selling price without current knowledge of the market. This action was not in your principal's best interests and therefore was unethical. After you learned from broker Stout what the lots were selling for, you should present the written offers but recommend to the owner that they not be accepted. You should relay the information that you received from broker Stout to Mr. Smith and suggest both a change in the listing based on more realistic value and a counteroffer.

12. Your real estate brokerage office is primarily engaged in the sale of single-family homes in the Crestwood area. Because you came across advantageous purchase opportunities, you also want to buy and sell homes in the Crestwood area. How can you ethically engage in selling property for others while you buy and sell similar property for yourself?

Owners who list property with your firm must have full knowledge that you are competing with them in that you are also selling your own property. You would also have to inform buyers which properties were owned by you and endeavor to present properties in such a manner as not to give preference to your own properties. When you buy property, if you share in a sales commission, you should inform the seller that not only are you a licensee, but that you are also buying for resale.

If you purchase a property that is either unlisted or listed by other brokers, and sell the property by listing it with other brokers, this would not be a breach of ethics. Of course, you would have to indicate clearly that you were dealing as a principal for the purpose of resale. By listing the property with another office, you can eliminate the problem of competing with your own principals.

If you act as a buyer's broker and buy similar property without first offering it to your buyer clients, you would be breaching your fiduciary relationship by personally competing with them.

13. A couple owns a house free and clear. A licensed salesperson presents an offer where the buyer was to give the seller $45,000 cash and a subordinate mortgage for the balance of the purchase price. (A subordinate loan places the loan in a junior position to loans placed against the property at a later date.) This offer allows the purchaser to obtain a $108,000 loan, from which the purchaser obtained the $45,000 down payment. This leaves the purchaser with $63,000 cash. Is there anything wrong with this arrangement?

Not only would the buyer take over the property without an investment, the buyer actually would receive $63,000 cash to buy the property. If the buyer defaulted, the sellers would not be able *to collect on the second mortgage and would be obligated to pay a $108,000 first mortgage or have the property foreclosed. Failure to protect a principal must be regarded as unethical conduct.*

If sellers indicate an interest in accepting an offer of this type, the agent should strongly recommend that they seek legal advice prior to their acceptance.

14. A buyer is a national corporation. The buyer's representative asks the listing agent not to reveal to the owner the buyer's true identity. If the agent complies with the buyer's request, will the agent have breached the fiduciary duty to the owner?

    Yes. The primary duty of the broker is to his or her principal. The agent has a duty to disclose to his or her principal any pertinent information the agent receives concerning the agency that was not received in confidence.

    If the agent was the buyer's agent, then it would be unethical to inform the seller of the buyer's identity, as it would be contrary to a lawful instruction of the agent's principal.

15. A broker offers a seller a rebate of a portion of the commission paid if the seller buys another property through the broker's office within a stated period of time. Is the broker's action unethical?

    Rebating a portion of the commission to the principal is, in effect, a reduced commission. Reducing a commission is not by itself unethical, even when tied to another purchase. An ethics problem might arise if the rebate is not offered to all similar sellers.

16. You elect to act as a dual agent representing both buyer and seller in a transaction (assuming such an agency election is proper in your state). Your office policy is to show your office listings first to prospective buyers. If you are unable to satisfy the buyers' needs with properties you have listed, then the policy is to show homes listed by brokerage firms offering a similar commission and commission split. You are only to show homes where reduced commissions would be received in cases where you are otherwise unable to meet buyer needs. Is there an ethical problem?

    Your office policy gives preference to your own listings that best serve the needs of the owners of your own listings. However, you wish to act in a dual agency capacity, which means that the best interests of the buyers must also be considered. Your office policy is based on your personal best interests and not the best interests of buyers. By this policy, you place self-interest above that of your clients while claiming to have an agency duty. This policy could be unethical without full disclosure to buyers that you will place their interests secondary to your own.

By having this office policy, you are likely engaged in illegal price fixing. Your actions also are likely to be an illegal restraint of trade.

17. You are a buyer's agent and show your prospective buyer client a home on which she wants to make an offer. The listing broker indicates that his firm cooperates fully with buyer's brokers and gives buyer's brokers the same commission split as they do for subagency. The listing broker also informs you that there is a $5,000 special bonus to the selling office for this property. What, if any are the ethical problems involved in this situation?

If you had shown the property while knowing of the special bonus and had not disclosed it to your buyer client, there would be a serious question as to self-serving actions rather than best meeting client needs. When you learned about the bonus, you had a duty to inform the buyers prior to any offer they would make. Ethically, you generally would have no duty to give the bonus to or split it with your client. Many buyer listings provide that when the listing office splits the commission with the broker, the buyer is relieved of paying the commission. There could be a problem if your buyer had agreed to make up any shortfall between your share of a cooperative-sale commission and the fee stated in your buyer-agency agreement. If the buyer is to be responsible for any shortfall, placing yourself in the buyer's position would seem to indicate that the buyer should have some interest in the bonus in the absence of any provision to the contrary in the listing contract.

3. Responsibilities to the Buyer

Disclosure + Fairness = A Satisfied Buyer

The doctrine of *caveat emptor*, literally, "let the buyer beware," once was the general rule in the business world. With the rise of consumerism in the last four decades, however, it has all but disappeared. Consumers want to make sure their interests are protected. This is not always as easy as it seems.

For example, the concept of buyer agency is now generally accepted. Even when the real estate licensee is the listing, and thus the seller's, agent, he or she still has obligations and duties to the buyer, who in this case would be a customer and not the agent's principal. Though no fiduciary duty may exist, there is always a duty of honest dealing.

When working with buyers, a seller's agent also has a duty to assist the buyers in meeting their needs. As a professional dealing mostly with novices, a licensee guides purchasers in what probably will be the greatest investment of their lives. This guidance could involve educating and counseling prospective buyers, as well as trying to locate properties that meet their needs. Agent-client and subagent-customer relationships are characterized in Table 3.1.

Table 3.1   Client and Customer Relationships

Agent-Client Relationship	Subagent-Customer Relationship
Liability for agent's actions	No liability for agent's actions
Agent works *for*	Subagent works *with*
Advocacy	No advocacy
Advice	No advice contrary to seller's interest
Duties include confidentiality, obedience, accounting, reasonable care and diligence, loyalty and full disclosure	Duties include fair and honest treatment and disclosure of known facts or facts subagent is expected to know

While a buyer's agent has relatively limited contact with sellers, a buyer's agent does have a duty of fair play toward sellers. In cases of buyer's agents, the seller really is the agent's customer. As an example, use of a purchase form that was intended to deceive a seller as to what was really being offered would be unethical behavior. The Golden Rule does not deal exclusively with seller's agents; it applies to everyone.

Inform the Buyer about Agency

As previously stated, confusion among members of the public about whom the broker represents is a serious problem in the real estate industry. The buyer must be informed as soon as possible, preferably during the initial qualifying of the buyer, about the agency relationship that the broker will have in working with the buyer, as well as duties the licensee has to the buyer.

Today, most brokers, in informing buyers about agency relationships, tell prospective buyers about buyer agency and give the buyer the choice of buyer agency. If chosen, the agent will represent the buyers, not the property owners. From an ethical point of view, it certainly passes the test of the Golden Rule. It should be pointed out that agency interests may be in conflict if a buyer agent shows property listed with his or her firm. Because of this potential conflict, some brokers elect to be only buyer's agents, in which case their office would not take listings, or they serve as seller's agents in an agency or subagency capacity. Another alternative, where allowed, is a consensual agreement with the buyers and sellers to serve as a dual agent.

Qualifying Buyers

When dealing with buyers, an agent has a duty to endeavor to understand the needs and desires of buyers and to then work to best meet the buyers' wishes. To do otherwise would be to waste the buyers' time.

Because the majority of real estate transactions require financing, the agent has an obligation to prequalify the buyers financially by using current lender requirements to determine the maximum debt that the buyers will be allowed to take on. Failure to qualify buyers financially could give them false hopes of what they are able to purchase and could waste months of house-hunting and negotiation time. To reduce the likelihood of financing problems after an offer has been accepted, many brokers will have a local lender prequalify prospective buyers for financing.

Failure to prequalify buyers could also be a breach of the sellers' agent's duty to the sellers. An offer from the buyers who cannot obtain financing could prolong the sale process and be detrimental to the sellers' interests. When an owner accepts an offer where the seller is unable to complete the purchase, the property is taken off the market for weeks at best, and at worse, for months. Possible buyers for the property could be lost to other properties.

Besides the loss of possible qualified buyers, the owner would also be subject to holding costs for a longer sale period. An owner could have also obligated him or herself to another purchase, believing that a sale had taken place. Another possible repercussion of acceptance of such an offer could be that the lengthy sale period created by the deal could then cause a seller, out of desperation, to accept an offer that is not in his or her best interests.

Unsuitable Property

An unethical act would be to show prospective buyers property that does not meet their needs, but is shown solely to indicate to owners that the agent is working to sell their property. This would be deceiving the owners as well as wasting the buyers' time. Such showings could not pass the test of the Golden Rule.

Overpriced Property

There would be an ethical problem in showing a buyer overpriced property when the purpose of showing the overpriced property was to give a buyer a false sense of property value. There is no ethical problem in such a showing if the purpose was simply to give the buyer a comprehensive view of what property was available in the marketplace or within a desired area that would meet the criteria set forth by the buyer.

There is nothing unethical about holding off showing what the agent believes to be the best property available if the purpose is to give the buyer a better understanding of the market. This could lead to greater appreciation of the final property shown. If, however, properties are selected to give a distorted view of the market or market values, or both, then such action would be deceitful and dishonest.

Duty of Full Disclosure

The licensee has the duty to disclose to a buyer any knowledge the agent has about a property that might be considered a material defect, such as termite infestation or structural defects. Note that the licensee also has an affirmative duty to discover those adverse factors that a reasonably competent and diligent investigation would disclose. Such factors should be disclosed to both buyer and seller.

Some states have mandated property disclosures by the seller or agent, or both, and have limited inspection duties to a visual inspection of readily accessible areas. There is generally no duty by the agent to discover and disclose latent or hidden defects.

The expertise required as to the agent's inspection should be based on the degree of knowledge expected of an agent by the state licensing authority.

An agent should be aware of "red flags," things that don't look quite right. An example would be a driveway coming straight to a house that has no garage. This should alert an agent that there was likely a garage that has been converted to part of the house. A prudent agent should check to see that any conversion work was performed with a building permit and that the conversion meets current state and local codes. Other common red flags would be obvious indications of water leaks or structural problems caused by various soil conditions.

While real estate professionals are not required to be construction or engineering experts, a diligent inspection nevertheless can reveal areas for concern. In most parts of the country, it is a common practice for the agent to recommend that the buyer make any offer subject to a professional home inspection. Generally, the agreement will allow the seller to make necessary corrections or, if unwilling, allow the buyer to set aside the agreement.

Many states now require sellers to disclose any adverse information they have as to the property. This disclosure may be a signed comprehensive form provided to the purchaser. While this book is about duties of real estate professionals, sellers of real property also have ethical duties, which, in many cases, have now become legal duties.

Selling without specifically pointing out negative information set forth in small print in the contracts also would be unethical. For example, one developer included in the small print the right to harvest the trees on the lots sold until the lots were fully paid for. This information was not disclosed in sales brochures or presentations. Most of the purchasers were unaware of the provision until they discovered their beautiful trees had been harvested.

In selling a cooperative unit or condominium, the broker must be familiar with the specific cooperative or condominium documents and must inform the buyer of any unusual restrictions or obligations therein. In a number of states, the real estate agent must deliver copies of the association bylaws and restrictions as well as supply information on assessments and any delinquencies.

Some condominium developers have created recreational leases whereby they retain ownership of the recreational facilities and rent them to the condominium association for an unrealistic fee. They accomplish this by signing the recreational lease while they still control the association. One such lease provided for a payment of $25,000 per month for a swimming pool. The lease information was included with the condominium association bylaws and regulations. Generally, buyers didn't discover this until after they had purchased. Then they asked questions about why their fees were so high. When a licensee handles the initial sale or resale of a property with a recreational lease, he or she has an ethical duty of full disclosure to the purchaser. (In several states, such as Michigan and New York, recreational leases are banned by law.)

If a licensee knows that the buyer's planned use for the property violates either a public or private restriction, the licensee must inform the buyer of the restrictions.

When property is leased, the licensee should make copies of the leases available to the purchaser, rather than providing selected information from the leases.

Buyers should fully understand who owns the appliances, if any services are being received in lieu of rent, the amount of lease deposits and so on. Place yourself in the buyer's shoes. If you would want to know this information, then you should supply it.

In some states, a property is reassessed for tax purposes when it is sold. Giving unsophisticated prospective buyers previous tax information might deceive them and, thus, would be unethical. The agent must explain that the property will be reassessed upon sale, which may increase property taxes.

Your duties to buyers are related to their levels of sophistication in real estate matters. In selling income property to an investor who buys and sells many properties, you probably would not have to explain that scheduled rents assume a 100 percent occupancy factor. However, if the purchaser is unsophisticated, buying his or her first investment property, the agent has a duty to explain that scheduled rents are based on 100 percent occupancy—which is unlikely—and that the purchaser should count on a vacancy factor as well as some collection loss.

Although the last vestiges of the doctrine of caveat emptor still hold in only a few states, the trend is to retain the agent as an expert source of information to both parties.

Hazardous Conditions

If a selling agent knows of any natural or manufactured problems concerning an area or property that likely would be regarded by a buyer as the type of information he or she would want to know, then the agent should make full disclosure of the problem.

If an area has had flood problems, you should make prospective buyers aware of the past problems. Of course, if work has since been done to solve the flood problems, such information can also be provided. In California, agents must disclose to buyers the fact that a property is within an earthquake (seismic) hazard area.

Because of serious problems that could be related to dump sites and landfill areas, a real estate professional should disclose any known land-fills within a reasonable area. If a home is known to have been built on filled land, this fact should be conveyed to the buyer. There could be dangers based on the nature of the fill from a hazardous substance standpoint as well as to the ability of the land to adequately support the structure.

If a property is located on or in close proximity to a former military ordnance facility where explosives or chemicals were stored or tested, the agent should disclose such facts if known.

If other property in the area has had problems with radon, a naturally occurring colorless and odorless gas that has been linked to lung cancer, the agent should disclose known facts to prospective purchasers. Prospective buyers should be advised of firms that can test for radon problems.

Asbestos is found mainly in the floor and ceiling tile, roofing, insulation and fire-proofing of structures built before 1970. It was often used to insulate furnaces, ducts and steam pipes as well. If the agent knows of or suspects the presence of asbestos, he or she should, of course, inform any prospective buyer.

Urea formaldehyde foam insulation was formerly used in walls and ceilings of homes and mobile homes. The gas emission from this insulation can be harmful. If its presence is known, the agent should inform any prospective buyer.

The presence of lead-based paint can result in lead poisoning and should of course be disclosed. Older properties had lead water lines. If an agent knows there are lead pipes, this fact should be made known to prospective buyers.

Electromagnetic fields are created by high-tension wires. While there is some controversy as to the danger of these fields, they have been related to a variety of ills, including cancer. The application of the Golden Rule would seem to dictate that the proximity of high-tension wires, as well as claimed problems associated with the lines, should be conveyed to buyers.

When a site has been used for commercial or industrial purposes where hazardous materials may have been used, the agent should inform the buyer of what he or she knows and suggest that the buyer secure an environmental study of the site. This problem is particularly acute in property that had underground storage tanks, such as former gas stations where soil has often been contaminated by leaking tanks. In cases of former gas stations, adjacent property might also have been contaminated.

In a number of states, sellers must disclose knowledge of hazard problems, including hazardous waste discharged on or that had been stored on the premises. Most commercial real estate transactions require a phase I environmental study. Even if your state does not require that the owner make any disclosures as to hazard problems, the listing agent should nevertheless question the owner as to any known problems and supply such information to cobrokers.

Again, while you are not expected to be a construction or environmental expert, you have a duty to use your expertise and to inquire about red flags. When in doubt, disclose.

Stigmatized Property

Stigmatized property is that which is made undesirable by reasons other than physical or environmental problems. Some property would be considered undesirable by prospective purchasers because someone lived on the property or something happened in the property.

In many states, the fact that a murder or suicide occurred on a property does not have to be disclosed as a matter of law. California law states that a murder or suicide need not be disclosed after three years. While you must be aware of your state laws, keep in mind that state laws set the minimum standards for all types of possible stigmas. Put yourself in a prospective purchaser's shoes to determine whether disclosure would be ethically required.

Finding out about a murder or suicide in a home after purchase could adversely affect a purchaser's perception and enjoyment of his or her new home, especially if the death was recent or highly publicized. Nightmares and nervous apprehension could affect adults as well as children. After learning of such problems, buyers have been known to resell or walk away from their homes. Logic tells us that a past murder or suicide should not matter. The home is the same regardless of what happened there. However, emotional reactions to negative events often defy logic. Withholding knowledge of a murder or suicide could result in emotionally, and possibly economically, harming the buyer.

By itself, death would generally not need to be disclosed. It would be normal for a home that is past the century mark to have had at least one death of an occupant. If, however, you had knowledge that a death in a house would be regarded as unlucky or otherwise a negative factor to a prospective buyer, then application of the Golden Rule could require you to disclose information you have as to a death that occurred on the property. For example, some cultural groups regard a death in a house as an unlucky omen.

The authors do not consider the fact that a prior owner had, or died of, AIDS or was HIV-positive as a problem that must be disclosed. Buildings do not transmit HIV or cause AIDS. People share hospitals, restaurants and workplaces with others who have AIDS or who are HIV-positive without contracting it themselves. It should be pointed out that if you disclose to a buyer that a former owner has AIDS or is HIV-positive and you are wrong, you could be liable for slander.

Because HIV is a gray area as to disclosure, a number of states have passed laws specifically exempting AIDS from state disclosure requirements. Keep in mind that those infected with the AIDS virus are also considered a protected class as a handicap under federal Civil Rights Law.

There are other factors that can stigmatize a house, such as a molestation or other crime that occurred on the property, satanic rituals that are known to have taken place on the property or even a series of burglaries or calamities that had befallen previous owners, making the house "unlucky." While there can be many gray areas, apply the Golden Rule to each case to help in determining a proper course of action.

A haunted house also could create a problem. While you might laugh at the idea of ghosts sharing a house, many people take the supernatural very seriously. If the purported presence of ghosts is well known within the community, then the application of the Golden Rule would seem to indicate that disclosure should be made.

Verify, Verify, Verify

A real estate licensee should not provide buyers with unsubstantiated information or estimates when verification is possible. Never guess!

The licensee cannot escape this duty by simply stating "Well, this is the information the owner gave me," or "I took the information from a previous listing."

The licensee has a duty to make certain that when information is given to a buyer it is not only accurate, but complete. For example, when selling an apartment or office building, the licensee has a duty to see that a realistic vacancy factor is used. If utility costs or taxes on the building were based on rates lower than are presently in effect, the licensee has a duty to point this out to the purchaser. Some operating statements on investment property indicate utility and fuel costs based on five-year or ten-year averages. Use of these averages must be regarded as unethical, because the usual purpose is to lower costs unrealistically by averaging in years when costs were lower. If averages are used, they should be average gallons of oil or cubic feet of gas and kilowatts of electricity consumed, with current rates applied to these quantities.

When selling a business, it is unethical for a licensee to quote profit figures unless they have been verified from the owner's tax returns. Note that it is not sufficient to check and quote only one year's prior records when other years are also available. It could be unethical to quote ballpark figures from memory when they could be researched and given exactly.

If a licensee makes a statement that some work will be done to the property before the sale, or that any item of personal property is to be included in the transaction, the licensee is obliged to ensure that it is written in the buyer's offer in a complete and precise fashion so that the buyer and seller have no doubt as to the agreement.

A licensee should not offer dollar estimates on repair costs without having either specific expertise in the field or professional written estimates.

Explaining the Agreement

The licensee has a duty to make sure that purchasers fully understand the purchase agreement as well as any other document before they sign it. The less sophisticated the buyer, the greater care the agent should use in explaining all provisions of the purchase contract. Be especially careful of people who do not understand English very well, have very little education or are illiterate, as well as those who appear to have a mental impairment. Also, be alert when dealing with very elderly and first-time buyers. If the agent is uncertain as to "informed consent," exp should be strongly recommended.

The licensee should make sure that the purchaser knows the meaning of items such as adjustable rate loans, acceleration clauses and so forth. If financing could be a problem, the licensee either should suggest an offer contingent on financing or point out the legal consequences if the loan is not obtained. As an expert, the licensee has a duty to understand local financing.

In a sale with balloon-payment financing, the buyer must understand fully what will happen if the balloon payment becomes due and new financing is then unavailable or too costly.

The agent should never discourage a buyer or seller from obtaining legal advice; in fact, such advice should be strongly recommended.

Protecting the Buyer's Deposit

While legal in some states, it could nevertheless be unethical to remit a buyer's deposit to an owner prior to closing without the buyer's express permission. The buyer must be protected at all times. In any transaction, the possibility exists that the seller, because of financial or other difficulties, might breach the contract and be unable to return the deposit. To protect the buyer's deposit, an offer should specify that the deposit will be placed in your separate trust account or in a neutral escrow account until closing. Licensees must keep in mind that even when they represent sellers, they nevertheless must make certain that the buyer is treated in a professional manner. (For further discussion of handling buyer deposits, see Chapter 7.)

In selling an uncompleted house, the licensee also has a duty to see that the buyer's down payment goes into a trust account or neutral escrow account and not directly to the builder. If the house is never finished, the buyer might never see the down payment again.

Avoiding Unethical Acts

Unethical behavior comes in many forms:

- Discrimination is unethical. All prospective buyers must be treated equally without regard to sex, race, color, religion, national origin, age, handicap or familial status. Discrimination based on familial status includes acts against buyers because they are parents, guardians or persons in the process of obtaining legal custody of persons under the age of 18, or pregnant. Just because discrimination is possibly allowable under the law does not make it ethical, because discrimination of any type can never pass the test of the Golden Rule. Overly qualifying or steering prospects, or not attempting to close a sale would be disparate treatment and cannot be condoned. Every person must be given equal service!

- Participating in a high-pressure sales program, such as one where customers who fail to buy are humiliated, must be regarded as unethical behavior.
- Suggestions that time-shares and undivided-interest developments are investments should not be made, since the likelihood of reasonable appreciation or even any appreciation or reasonable return on the "investment" within a foreseeable future is relatively obscure.
- It would be unprofessional for a licensee to use a standard residential contract for a complex sale of nonresidential property. It would be unethical, of course, for a broker to write up any offer that is beyond his or her experience or expertise. When entering into complex agreements, the licensee should suggest that the buyer be represented by legal counsel.
- It could be unethical for a licensee to write up a land contract agreement that does not give the purchaser the right to record or obtain clear title. Likewise, it would be unethical to handle a land contract sale that includes a blanket encumbrance over several properties in a subdivision with no provision that ensures the purchaser can obtain clear title when the contract is paid.
- Encouraging or consenting through silence to fraud on a mortgage application could be a violation of federal law, as well as being unethical conduct.
- It would be unethical to ask a buyer to sign any disclosure report required by law without telling him or her to read it first. It also would be unethical to advise a buyer to ignore governmental or other regulations or to indicate how they could be evaded. For example, it would be unethical to help the buyer avoid Federal Housing Administration (FHA) or Department of Veterans Affairs (VA) restrictions on secondary financing by suggesting loans to

finance the down payment. In addition, it would be unethical to write up a second, false contract to set a higher valuation for financing or to show a greater down payment, or to otherwise deceive. This type of conduct generally would be regarded as fraud and could subject an agent to civil penalties as well as possible criminal penalties.

- Including fine print in a contract naming the escrow or attorney for closing is unethical. The right of the broker to decide this matter applies only in cases where the principals fail to specify a preference. Likewise, it would be unethical to suggest a specific financing, title company or any other service where the licensee would obtain a gratuity or kickback in any form, unless the buyer and seller are aware of this and specifically agree to the arrangement. In most states, such kickbacks are also illegal.

- Placing a prelisting agreement in an offer whereby the buyer agrees to list with the broker whenever the property is again placed on the market is unethical. This stipulation would not be in the best interests of the seller, because the commitment could serve to discourage buyers and, because the buyer might forget about the provision, it could be a source of controversy. Brokers who use these stipulations are overreaching for future commissions and placing their own interests before those of their clients. This would be a very risky conflict of interest.

- If the property is new, it could be unethical to include in an offer a provision that relieves the builder or seller of responsibility for any defects involving the premises, unless such a provision is specifically stated and set forth in bold print. The consequence of this type of provision is that the buyer is giving up legal rights, and this amounts to an "as is" contract, which generally should be avoided. "As is" clauses provide that the seller will not be liable for any physical defects in the property. If such a clause is used, it should apply only to specific, known problems. Some attorneys consider "as is" contracts unethical. Some states require by law that a builder warrant a new house for a designated period of time, such as one year, so state law could void any provision limiting the builder's warranty.

- It would be unethical to delay an interested buyer until a listing expires so that a licensee could get the full commission by negotiating a new listing, thus becoming both the listing and selling broker. This is not fair to the buyer, since the property might be sold before he or she has an opportunity to purchase it.

- Indicating a false sense of urgency by mentioning expected offers, another buyer or showing and so on when none exists also would be unethical. It would not be unethical, however, to indicate urgency based on fact.

- Using subterfuge to bring in prospective buyers is, of course, unethical. One land developer sold lots out of a building in Las Vegas, Nevada, with signs that read, "Official Las Vegas Welcoming Center," when in fact such a "center" did not exist.

- It could be unethical for a licensee to recommend that a customer purchase or rent a property when the licensee knows that the buyer or renter cannot make the payments.

- If prospective purchasers want an independent fee appraisal, a termite or structural inspection or a legal review of the purchase contract, it would be unethical to discourage them from seeking this expert professional help. To do so would be discouraging what would be in their best interests. It would also be in your best interest if professional help is obtained, as it reduces the likelihood that a purchaser will later claim that you were not honest in your representation of the property or that you provided improper advice.

- When driving prospective buyers to a property, some agents will choose a roundabout route that portrays the destination area in a more positive light. Although this practice in itself is not unethical, intentionally avoiding passing by aesthetically unattractive properties in the immediate area or neighborhood is unethical because the licensee would be concealing detrimental information about the area in which the property is located.

- It would be unethical to show prospective buyers property where the purpose is not to sell, but to show the seller you are working on selling the property. This deceives the owners and wastes the time of prospective buyers, who want to see property that meets their needs.

- It would be unethical, when showing multifamily units for sale, to show only units that are in better repair than most, or units that have recently been upgraded. Unless he or she specifically states otherwise, the licensee would be implying that the units shown are representative of all units for sale. Failing to show less desirable units could be negative fraud. The licensee must avoid misrepresentation by omission.

- Although self-confidence is good, the licensee must not appear positive when he or she is actually not sure. It is fraud to make a statement as fact when it is not known to be fact in order to induce a buyer to purchase.
- An agent should make no representations that cannot be made from the agent's own knowledge, unless the agent identifies the source of the information. Without knowledge, the only correct answer to a buyer's inquiry should be, "I don't know, but I'll make a point of finding out," or "I suggest you check with your [attorney] [accountant]."
- If, after a sales contract has been signed, you discover you have given a prospective buyer false information, you have an ethical as well as a legal duty to inform the buyer and the seller immediately of the facts. You must do this even though you may have believed at the time that the incorrect information was true. It may be embarrassing, but it must be done. Failure to do so could be fraud on your part.
- If, in the previous case, you discover that the seller had given you or the buyer false information with the apparent intent to deceive the buyer, you also have the duty to fully inform the buyer of the facts. Your duty to your principal does not include helping him or her take wrongful advantage of a purchaser.
- It would be unethical for a licensee to repeat to the buyer or seller personal information received in expressed or implied confidence from either party. This could also be a breach of fiduciary duty.

Examples of Deceit

Some unethical behavior stems from business practices that are patently deceitful. Some examples follow:

- In the past, some land salespeople used shills, or decoys, who pretended to be buyers. Prospective purchasers were paired off with shills who related well to the prospects. The shills get enthused about the property, sign purchase contracts to buy and try to get the other couple to buy. Using shills cannot be condoned; it is pure fraud.

- In advertising for a California land project, one developer combined the torrid 100 °F-plus summer temperatures and below-freezing winter temperatures to advertise a pleasant average annual temperature of 75 °F. Although technically true, the "average" temperature as presented was deceptive.
- Several land developments have claimed that the nationally known celebrities doing their commercials were purchasers. In some cases, the celebrities were given properties as payment for their services or they were allowed to purchase properties at below-market prices. This is really deceit because a viewer would imagine that the celebrity chose the development when in reality the celebrity was chosen by the developer.
- In large developments, Sold signs are frequently placed on new homes and lots that are not yet sold. Often an agent will suggest to prospective buyers that the agent place a Sold sign on a property to "hold it" for them. The use of Sold signs for unsold property is unethical. It deceives prospective buyers into a false sense of urgency.

Most real estate swindles, however, are not necessarily violations of the law. They are often sales at ridiculous prices. The sellers get into trouble with the law when they make false representations about value, use or future improvements.

Offering a property for sale at a price that is far higher than its worth creates an ethical dilemma. Certainly an agent has a duty to get the best deal possible for an owner. Does this duty extend to obtaining a price that far exceeds market value? When an agent quotes a price to a buyer, does the agent represent that the price is within the realm of reality? Obviously, gray areas exist, but the authors believe that offering property for sale carries with it the implication that the price offered bears enough of a relationship to market value, that it will not shock the conscience of an informed buyer. Overpricing properties in an attempt to snare uninformed or naïve purchasers for extraordinary windfalls must be regarded as unethical if the Golden Rule is applied. By accepting such listings, an agent could be helping owners take unconscionable advantage of buyers.

An example of prices that bore no relationship to value was a Florida development where lots were sold at $5,000 each. The developer challenged the county tax assessment of $1,600 each and claimed the value of each lot was only $185.

In another case, a subdivider couldn't sell lots, which were priced at $600 per lot. He raised the price to $800 and, 60 days later, to $1,000 per lot. The sales presentation he used, with success, was that if you had purchased a lot four months ago, you already would have made $400. He created the illusion of enormous profit, when in fact the only profits were his own.

Kickbacks

Kickbacks are anything of value given by a provider of goods or services solely for a referral. While some state laws allow kickbacks to brokers, if the kickbacks are revealed to the parties involved, the federal Real Estate Settlement Procedures Act (RESPA) makes kickbacks by federally related lenders an illegal act. The reason kickbacks are prohibited is that borrowers might otherwise be directed to a particular lender based upon the benefits to be received by the broker rather than the best interests of the borrower. This aspect of RESPA is, therefore, a consumer protection measure.

According to HUD, many brokers and lenders have been prosecuted for using schemes to get around the anti-kickback provisions of RESPA. In some cases, brokers rented space within their offices to lenders at a high rent; often the space was never used. Other lenders picked up advertising costs for brokers. A more sophisticated approach has been to pay for broker's consulting fees, although little or no consulting actually took place. A gray area has been lenders placing cooperating brokers on their Board of Directors so that they could be paid generously for meetings and expenses.

HUD regards all such attempts, at skirting the purpose of the law, as being illegal. The purpose of the law is to assure that a borrower is not directed to a lender based upon other than the best interests of the borrower. Attempts to receive lender compensation for loan referrals must be regarded as unethical conduct—even when such action may have been initiated by the lender rather than the broker.

How To Protect Buyers

When you are the agent of the seller and the buyer is your customer, the best protection for buyers is for you, as a real estate professional, to observe the Golden Rule in your dealings with them. You must also be diligent as to what is happening around you. To fail to report wrongdoings of others is to condone wrongful acts.

In many states, a portion of real estate license fees goes into a recovery or guarantee fund. The purpose of these funds is to reimburse members of the public who suffer losses due to the wrongful acts of licensees. This is a positive example of the licensees in the real estate profession taking upon themselves the responsibility for the wrongful actions of a few. Encouraging state legislation to establish and maintain adequate funds, if such funds are not currently available, will do a great deal to improve the public image of the entire real estate profession and to protect buyers and sellers alike from the wrongful actions of a few unethical real estate licensees.

Case Study: The Salesperson Who Knew Too Much

Salesperson Wong kept a tape recorder on the front seat of his car. He used the recorder to record ideas and data on properties. Each night he would go through the recorded comments and enter items in his daily planner, write letters or make notations on listings if appropriate. When reviewing his daily tapes, Wong realized that he must have inadvertently turned his recorder on when he left the car to make a telephone call while showing listings to prospects that day. The conversation indicated that his prospective buyers were excited about a property they had seen and that unless they found something they liked better that day, they would put in an offer of $185,000 on the house. If the owner countered, they would accept the counteroffer because they were willing to pay up to the list price of $210,000. The prospects had made a $185,000 offer on the house they had indicated an interest in, and Wong was scheduled to meet with the owners to present the offer in about one hour. What should Wong do?

Analysis

As soon as he realized that the conversation was not his, Wong should have stopped listening and erased that portion of the tape. Continuing to listen to what was clearly a private conversation has to be considered unethical. The question is, however, what does Wong do now?

Regardless of the type of agency involved, Wong should contact the prospective buyers and tell them about the tape. He could also tell the buyers that his discovery of their intentions was tantamount to having received the information in confidence. Therefore, he could not reveal it to the sellers because to do so would breach that confidence. Wong also could tell the buyers that if they were uncomfortable with this, they could revoke their offer any time prior to acceptance.

If Wong represented the sellers as a sellers' agent or a dual agent, he should tell the sellers that he inadvertently recorded a private conversation of the buyers relating to the offer. In effect, he was eavesdropping on to the recording, so he could not reveal any part of the conversation.

If the information had come to Wong from another source, such as a remark by a friend of the buyers, then if Wong represented the owners, he would have a duty to disclose the information to the owners.

Ethics Questions

1. In showing a property, you specifically point out to the prospective buyers that the third bedroom had been added without a permit. You also tell them that taxes were $1,120. After the sale, the purchasers notify you that the city has ordered the addition to be removed because it does not meet the local codes. Taxes were also $1,680, not the $1,120 that they had been two years before. What, if anything, should you have done differently?

   Even though you told the buyers the bedroom had been added without a permit, they had reason to expect they could use it. You had a duty either to ascertain the extent of code violations; inform the buyers and warn them about possible actions; or strongly recommend that they seek professional help from a contractor and an attorney prior to making an offer.

   In supplying the tax figure, you had a duty to make sure that it was the latest available. You could have provided the buyers with the tax rate and estimates of taxes, based on reevaluation if you felt the present evaluation was too low or have otherwise indicated that the taxes would likely increase.

   In some states, property is reassessed for taxes upon sale based on the sale price. If this is the case in your area, you should have explained this to the buyers. You should not give purchasers the impression that taxes are static.

2. While you're driving a prospect through an area, the customer spots a beautiful colonial home and exclaims, "Now, if you had that house for $140,000, I would jump at it." The house indicated was listed earlier that day for $129,500. You know that a truck terminal is planned across the road, which happens to be zoned commercial. You also know that ten years earlier, a wife murdered her husband in the living room and then committed suicide. What course of action should you take?

   You should explain to the prospect that the house was listed at $129,500. You also should provide the known adverse material facts you possess. Failure to provide this information would be unethical, because such facts might influence the decisions of many prospects.

Some states do not require you to disclose murder or suicide after a stated period of time; however, states deal with legal, not ethical, considerations. Apply the Golden Rule. As a prospective buyer, would you want to know of a murder-suicide in the home you contemplated purchasing? While it is usually the buyer's agent who has the disclosure duty, this duty probably applies to seller agents as well, even when the law specifies that disclosure need not be made, especially if the murder-suicide was common knowledge, particularly brutal and widely publicized. If the listing agent intended to disclose murder or suicide in the property, then the listing agent should inform the owner that such disclosures will be made. All licensees should be familiar with their state laws concerning stigmatized property.

3. You show a small home. The seller, an investor, had purchased a number of such properties at foreclosure sales and has made cosmetic repairs only. Other buyers have already discovered serious problems with the other homes. You know of nothing specifically detrimental regarding this property. What should you do if your prospect wishes to place an offer?

    Although you don't know of any faults concerning this property, you should inform the buyer of the problems others are experiencing. Suggest that the buyer have the house's structural, plumbing, heating, cooling and electrical work thoroughly checked. You should strongly recommend that the offer include the buyer's request for an inspection by an expert, with the owner given the option either to make repairs indicated by the inspection or to cancel the sale. Many standard contract forms include this type of inspection clause.

    If the owner's repairs in the past were designed to conceal faults, you should convey known facts to the buyer and strongly recommend that the buyer obtain professional home inspection as well as legal advice. You could be a participant in fraud if all appropriate disclosures were not made. You could also ethically refuse to represent such an owner.

4. You are unaware of any county ordinance prohibiting mobile homes. A prospective buyer asks you if he can place a mobile home on a five-acre rural parcel that you have for sale. There are several mobile homes in the area. You know of one that was put in last month only

about a mile away. You reply, "No problem at all; this isn't the city. Out here, you can pretty much do as you want on your land so long as you don't interfere with your neighbors' rights." After purchasing, the buyer discovers that mobile homes can only be set up in mobile home parks or on parcels of ten acres or more.

The buyer comes to you and asks what you are going to do about it. What do you tell the buyer?

You really made a guaranty when you told the purchaser that a mobile home could be placed on the property. As an expert, you should have checked before giving a definite answer. You now have the duty to rectify the situation.

Solutions include:

a. *Offer to buy the property yourself.*
b. *Offer to handle the resale of the property and indemnify the owner for any loss.*
c. *Offer a sum of money as damages.*
d. *Offer to arbitrate the matter if a satisfactory settlement cannot be reached.*

You can see that making positive guaranties or promises can be expensive if you don't check your facts. Don't make unverified assumptions.

5. A couple is looking for a site for a retirement home in an undeveloped area. You show them a lovely lake-view, wooded homesite. They immediately fall in love with the site. They purchase it and then discover that they cannot build on it because it will not pass a percolation test for septic systems. You only showed the site, pointed out the boundaries and quoted the price. You never even considered septic systems. Did you do anything wrong? If so, what?

You knew the buyers wanted to build on the site and that, in the absence of sewers, a percolation test would be required prior to obtaining a building permit. You are an expert; you should have suggested an offer contingent on the property passing a percolation test. Not even considering the problem shows that you were negligent. You have an ethical duty to "make it right."

6. You obtain a listing from Donna Smith, a real estate speculator. You estimate the property to be worth $90,000, but you list it at $210,000. Ms. Smith tells you the price is firm, because she figures

an out-of-town buyer, who doesn't know how low the local values are, will come along and buy it. Sure enough, an out-of-town couple comes to your office and you show and sell them the Smith property. After the sale, they come to you angry because they overpaid. You tell them you are sorry, but you are only an agent and, furthermore, you never told them the price was fair. Is your position valid? Why?

You should never have taken the listing. Ms. Smith wanted to take advantage of an ignorant buyer, and you agreed to help. Normally, your duty is to obtain the best deal possible for the owner, but this doesn't apply in a case where the owner wants to take advantage of an uninformed buyer and is not interested in a fair price. Bear in mind that in listing a property at a particular price, you are in essence stating to buyers that you do not consider the price asked to be unconscionable. Exactly what is "unconscionable" is a gray area that is best determined by the application of the Golden Rule.

7. Mrs. Connelly asks you to help her find land in a particular area. She confides in you that a large manufacturer will announce a new plant in the area in the near future. You help her find several parcels, which she buys, and she pays you a fee as a buyer's agent for locating these parcels. You find another large parcel for sale, upon which you obtain an option to buy. You offer to sell the option to Mrs. Connelly. Mrs. Connelly is delighted with the price you obtained and considers it an excellent deal. She then purchases your option for $14,000.
   You consider your ethics above reproach. Are they?

   You represented Mrs. Connelly and, therefore, you had a duty not to compete with her. In obtaining the option, you acted as principal. Even though Mrs. Connelly is happy, your action was unethical.

8. You receive a letter from Colonel Wilson, who is in Japan. Mrs. Wilson will be arriving in town in a few days, and his letter states, "I wish to engage your services as our agent to find suitable housing at a fair price for my family." When Mrs. Wilson arrives, you show her one of your listings, which she wants. You write up the offer and it is accepted. Since you obtain a commission on the sale of the house, you feel it would be unethical to charge the Wilsons, so you never submit a bill.

After Colonel Wilson arrives, he discovers termites in the house. You had not requested a termite inspection, although termites are occasionally found in the area. Colonel Wilson also discovers that a friend of his had previously looked at the property, and you had told the friend that the listing price, which Colonel Wilson paid, was "soft." You had said the place could be obtained for $7,000 to $11,000 less. When Colonel Wilson storms into your office, you inform him that the price he paid was fair and that you had comparables to back this up. Furthermore, you say you did not serve as his agent because you did not charge him for your services. You state that you represented the sellers and you had a duty to get the best deal for them. As for the termites, you did not know of them or you surely would have pointed out the problem. Are there any ethical problems here? If so, what are they?

Colonel Wilson was under the impression that you would represent him. You never informed him to the contrary, so it was implied that you were his agent. As such, you had a duty to obtain the best deal possible for him and to protect him. As an expert, you should have requested a termite inspection. You cannot avoid your responsibility by not charging Colonel Wilson.

You acted for both parties without their mutual consent. There was an undisclosed dual agency. You can avoid problems such as this by clearly informing buyer and seller in writing of your agency relationship and having them sign a statement that makes it clear that they give informed consent to the agency relationship.

If you were not to act as Colonel Wilson's agent, you should have contacted him and informed him of your agency selection and why you did so prior to taking the offer from Mrs. Wilson.

You could have elected to be a dual agent with the consent of the buyer and seller, but in a case such as this, handling a dual agency and being fair to both buyer and seller becomes very difficult.

When you told Colonel Wilson's friend that the price was soft, you violated a fiduciary duty to the owner unless the owner gave you permission to make such a disclosure.

9. You have a real estate agency and also possess an insurance broker's license. On each home sale, you say to the buyer, "I would recom-

mend you put a homeowner's policy on the property. To save you the bother, we would be happy to handle this for you and get you a really good deal." You write the policy through your own agency unless the buyer objects and wishes to place insurance with another agent. Is your action ethical?

Your behavior is unethical. You have a duty to inform the buyer that you have your own insurance agency. You imply that you are acting on the buyer's behalf when, in fact, a primary concern is earning an insurance commission. This is a very clear conflict of interest.

10. A manufacturer of modular homes offers its dealers special furniture packages. The furniture is scaled down by about 15 percent in order to make the rooms and the homes appear larger than they actually are. As an agent you are asked to sell from one of these furnished models. Is there an ethical problem?

    If you sell from these model homes without fully disclosing that the buyers' furniture will look different because the furniture is downsized, you would be guilty of deceit. You cannot excuse the deceit because the dealer did it. You know something detrimental so you must disclose it.

11. A prospective buyer is considering borrowing the down payment and assuming a loan on a home that you have listed. You have strong doubts about the buyer's ability to make the necessary payments. Do you press the buyer for an offer?

    You should make certain that the buyer fully understands the financial requirements of paying on the borrowed down payment as well as the payments on the loan being assumed. With this understanding, you should treat the buyer as you would any other buyer.
    You should inform the seller of the buyer's financial situation, as a buyer who defaults on a loan being assumed could result in negative information being recorded in a seller's credit file. In some states, deficiency judgments are possible, which means that the seller could be liable for a loss suffered by the lender should a foreclosure sale yield less than the balance due on the loan. If a deficiency judgment is possible, you would have to explain defi-

ciency judgments to the seller if you are a seller's agent or dual agent.

12. You are approached by Stupendous Properties to sell limited partnership interests in an industrial center. They offer you 20 percent commission on all sales and provide you with slick sales brochures.

   You contact buyers you have worked with on investment properties and are able to sell a number of the limited partnerships. The investments later sour and your buyers lose their entire investment. It is discovered that the general partners had used a wholly owned corporation to buy the property that they then resold to the partnership at a huge markup. What had appeared to be relatively conservative leverage of 40 to 50 percent turned out to be no-equity investments, because the property loans exceeded the market value of the property and projected income was overly optimistic. The actual income could not cover the debt service.

   Your local real estate organization has received an ethics complaint as to your actions. Did you act in a proper manner?

   The 20 percent commission should have alerted you to the fact that the price being paid for partnership interests was inflated and that the property would likely require significant appreciation in value to be worth what was being paid.

   Ethically, you cannot take the position that you are just the sales agent of these limited partnership securities and excuse your actions because it wasn't you who defrauded the investors. By representing the limited partnerships as investments, you had a duty of fair dealing to buyers. As a minimum, you should have checked to see if the general partner had any prior problems and the results of any other limited partnerships the general partner had been involved in. In this case, because of the high commission, you should have been alerted to do more. This should have been another red flag.

   You could have checked the value of the property by contacting industrial brokers in the area where it was located and asked for opinions based on the value and income indicated by Stupendous Properties. You should not have contacted prospective buyers until you had assured yourself as to the viability of the partnership as an investment.

13. You are eating in a restaurant and overhear a conversation in the next booth. One of the persons has just purchased an old country home on several acres. It seems that there are a number of large black walnut trees on the property worth close to $100,000 because of their suitability for veneer use. The party indicates he will cut down and sell the trees as soon as escrow closes and then default on the loan because a deficiency judgment is not possible in your state in cases of seller financing.

When the party leaves the restaurant, you realized he is your buyer, who is under a buyer agency agreement. You just sold him the property he described. The purchase price was $150,000 with $10,000 down and your buyer agreed to pay the balance of the purchase price within 12 months. The closing is scheduled for next week. What do you do?

You realize that your principal intends to use the law to defraud the seller. It is fraud, since the buyer does not intend to honor the agreement. While you are a buyer's agent and have a fiduciary duty to the buyer, you also have a duty of fair dealing to the seller. You should contact your principal and tell him what you overheard and what you will do. You should then contact the seller's agent and relay the information you have as to the buyer's intentions. If the seller was not represented by an agent, you should contact the seller directly.

If the buyer did not indicate that he or she intended to default on the loan, you would have no duty to inform the seller about the claimed value of the walnut trees.

If you had been a seller's agent, you would have to tell the seller about the claimed value of the walnut trees even though an offer had been accepted.

A real estate agent is not expected to be a timber expert, and has no legal or ethical duty to determine value of trees unless he or she makes representations as to their value.

14. Brokers approved by the Department of Housing and Urban Development (HUD) are allowed to submit more than one bid on a foreclosed property. Broker Able submits an offer from Mrs. Baker on a property. Assume that Mr. Charles contacts broker Able prior to the bid opening and asks to see the property. Should Able show

the property to Mr. Charles? Should Mr. Charles be told about the offer from Mrs. Baker?

If broker Able is acting as a seller's agent or dual agent, Able has a duty to show the property to Mr. Charles and to accept an offer if possible. Able cannot tell Mr. Charles details about Mrs. Baker's offer, as this would give Mr. Charles an unfair advantage over Mrs. Baker. Mrs. Baker also is entitled to have the details of the offer kept confidential as to other parties.

4. Responsibilities to the General Public

Regard for Community and Profession = Ethical, Sound Business Practices

---

Protecting the Community

By the very nature of their business, real estate licensees have a greater control over the formation and character of a community than does any other group. They therefore have a duty to be community-oriented. Licensees should contribute time and money to worthwhile community causes, listen to their neighbors and peers and respond to the needs and interests of the community at large. They also must express their ideas of right and wrong to the community. If otherwise unable to prevent ethical abuses, licensees should support legislation that would, in effect, make illegal what they consider unethical. An agent's duty to help eliminate fraud is clearly set forth in the preamble of the Code of Ethics and Standards of Practice of the National Association of REALTORS®:

> "They [REALTORS®] should identify and take steps, through enforcement of this Code of Ethics and by assisting appropriate regulatory bodies, to eliminate practices which may

damage the public or which might discredit or bring dishonor to the real estate profession."

Supporting Community Planning

Specifically, licensees should support proper community planning in order to help make the community a better place for all. For example, while striving to expand the local housing market, licensees should work with their community for controlled growth to ensure adequate infrastructure and services for residents.

Opposing Detrimental Land Use

Licensees should oppose certain land uses in areas where such uses would be detrimental to the general good of the community, even if they are allowed by local zoning ordinances. For example, a licensee might wish to oppose moving a busy truck terminal next to a grade school because of the inherent danger to the children's safety.

There is great satisfaction in seeing that land is put to its highest and best use and in knowing that you played an important part in its planning and development. To protect the best interests of their communities, licensees should oppose the premature formation of land sale subdivisions for speculative purposes. Such premature subdivisions fragment ownership of the land long before it is actually ready for development. Premature subdivision frustrates later proper land development. Often, the result is a rural slum. Breaking up huge tracts of land without regard for housing needs also tends to artificially inflate prices of surrounding land, drive up taxes, cause disorderly growth and prematurely takes land out of beneficial use.

Putting the Community First

When the interests of the community conflict with the interests of the real estate profession, the community's interests should come first. What is right is not always clear. Evaluating the ethics of a situation can be difficult. The correctness of an action depends on its motives and on results.

Growth Control and Equal Opportunity

Supporting growth control could be either ethical or unethical conduct. If your reason for supporting the measure is to protect the environment, it could well be laudable. If, however, the goals are to increase the value of developed property by limiting the supply or to keep minorities out of the area, then the action would be unethical. Similarly, large-lot requirements could help prevent congestion and pollution associated with high density, but they would also serve to keep prices high and minorities out.

Influencing Legislation

In the past, some broker groups vigorously fought fair housing legislation; this activity tended to lower the status of brokers in the public eye. At present, some broker organizations, as a matter of course, oppose all bond issues, tax increases and any other legislation that, they fear, may adversely affect the real estate profession. Blanket opposition to such legislation without regard for community needs is difficult to justify; however, opposing bond issues in the belief that there are more appropriate ways to finance the improvements, or in the belief that the improvements are not necessary, would not be unethical. Brokers should respond to proposed legislation with the community's interests in mind, and vigorously oppose any legislation that works to the detriment of their community.

Rent Control

As we've said, there is nothing unethical in influencing legislation for the proper reasons. For example, rent control generally is opposed by the real estate profession because the legislation virtually guarantees rental shortages, discourages the construction of new units by limiting future rent increases, encourages the demolition of units for redevelopment to other uses and encourages the conversion to condominiums. Rent control also tends to discourage home ownership—with below-market rent. Renters resist becoming buyers, which, in the long run, may work against their best financial interests. When tenants are, in effect, subsidized by property owners, they are hesitant to move, which makes it difficult for newcomers to obtain housing; this creates a virtual housing gridlock. Supporting rent control so that your rent remains low at the expense of others would have to be considered unethical conduct.

There are situations where the market forces of supply and demand are not present. As an example, many mobile homes cannot be economically relocated. Some mobile home park owners have taken advantage of this fact by increasing the rent significantly—increases that are not related to market rents being asked by other parks that have vacancies. Therefore, supporting rent control to prevent the exploitation of mobile home owners by a park management could be viewed as ethical conduct.

Protecting the Profession's Image

Licensees have a duty not only to conduct their business ethically and to adhere to the Golden Rule, but also to be aware of and to take action against practices of others that may have a detrimental effect on the public's opinion of brokers.

Real estate licensees have a duty to their profession to conduct their affairs in such a manner as to suggest not even a hint of impropriety. To do otherwise would not only result in negative public reaction to the individual and firm involved, it also would negatively affect the reputation of the entire real estate profession. Appearances do count!

Upgrading Standards

Many licensees do not belong to professional organizations, read professional journals or take advantage of professional training opportunities. Failing to strive for greater and current knowledge means that you may fail to best meet the needs of buyers, sellers and the general public.

The importance of striving for current information is stated thus in the preamble to the REALTORS® Code of Ethics:

> "In recognition and appreciation of their obligations to clients, customers, the public, and each other, REALTORS® continuously strive to become and remain informed on issues affecting real estate and, as knowledgeable professionals, they willingly share the fruit of their experience and study with others."

Failure to keep current on new regulations, laws and duties could also lead to a violation that could subject you to disciplinary action or financial liability, or both.

Finishing What You Start

Many people regard anyone engaged in real estate activities as being a representative of the real estate profession. As a result, the profession often takes the blame for actions of private investors and developers.

The image of brokers has been hurt by those who have started undercapitalized construction projects with only a "hope" of obtaining the rest of the needed capital. All too often, the result has been unfinished projects that remain community eyesores for years. Such conduct has long been regarded as unethical. Real estate licensees should avoid involvement in such ventures.

The credibility of real estate brokers and developers has been hurt by announcements of "magnificent" projects that fail to progress beyond the press-release-and-billboard stage. If a broker or developer believed he or she could put the project together and thought the publicity would help the project succeed, then these actions would be proper—optimism, by itself, is not unethical. Announcements of major developments, however, have tended to increase property value and sales activity in the areas of the planned developments. If an announcement of a project was made in order to market property at a higher price without the intention of fulfilling the announced plans, then this announcement would have to be viewed as unethical, as the purpose was to profit from others based on deceit.

Avoiding Unethical Influence

Many brokers and trade groups make political contributions. There is nothing unethical in helping a person get elected if you agree with his or her policies and the policies are not in themselves unethical. However, if the contributions are based on an agreement to take a particular voting position, then the contributions would be in effect bribes, which, of course, would be unethical.

In a few publicized cases, licensees were accused of bribing Federal Housing Authority (FHA) appraisers in order to receive favorable appraisals. In a highly publicized case, a large real estate development company was accused of influencing planning decisions. The accusations against the company included the following:

- Hiring a city mayor as its public relations representative
- Hiring a county planning director off the public payroll
- Hiring a district attorney to serve as its attorney in another county
- Giving a county supervisor free ads for his restaurant in a company paper
- Purchasing all its automobiles through a county supervisor's agency
- Purchasing insurance through another supervisor's agency

Although this development company's actions might have been entirely innocent and free of any attempt to improperly influence planning decisions, the company nevertheless allowed the appearance of blatantly attempting to do so. Without any other wrongdoing, this must be regarded as improper conduct because it reflects negatively on every real estate licensee.

Public Service

A problem affecting local and state business regulatory agencies is whether those who are the regulated should act as regulators. Some people feel that the control of a board by the profession or trade it is supposed to regulate is a conflict of interest. In some cases, boards have achieved a reputation for responding more to these special interests than to the public's interests. Many people, however, feel it is important to have people who are knowledgeable about the profession serving on regulatory boards. One solution to this apparent conflict would be to have more a mix of public members and real estate professionals on regulatory boards. To the credit of the real estate profession, we are seeing many cases where real estate professionals want to be harder on transgressors than do regulatory board members who are not real estate professionals.

A licensee serving on a professional regulatory board has a duty to avoid even the hint of improper action. For example, if a member of a regulatory board takes a position with a firm after that member was involved in a favorable ruling concerning that firm, this would appear to be improper behavior. In the same manner, if that firm hires a close family member of the board member after a favorable ruling or while a significant matter was pending, it would also create the appearance of impropriety. Even if the board member is blameless, failing to work to avoid the appearance of unethical conduct could in itself be unethical because it would reflect badly on the entire real estate profession.

It would be improper for a licensee to violate the confidentiality of information he or she received while acting in a position of public trust. As an example, assume a licensee served on a local planning commission and told a friend about a likely rezoning that was not yet public knowledge and suggested that the friend contact owners of properties in the area and make purchase offers, since the value of the property would increase dramatically once the zoning changes were announced. If the friend purchased property based on the insider information and profited, the agent's disclosure would have to be regarded as improper even though the agent did not share in the profit. The agent gave a friend knowledge that was used to the detriment of an owner, who sold without the benefit of the inside information. This clearly violates the public trust and in many states is illegal.

Avoiding Unethical Acts

Fraud

Many of the real estate profession's image problems stem, not from licensees acting as agents, but from licensees acting as principals. For example, in November 1975, a federal grand jury handed down an indictment charging that one real estate company had sold 77,000 semi-arid and desert lots to unsuspecting consumers. The land company originally paid $17.8 million for the land and improvements, yet sold the lots for more than $200 million. Improvements made to the property were of the showcase variety; few lots had water, sewers or electricity, or the hope of ever getting any. Free dinners and drinks were used to lure consumers to the "investment seminars." Once there, the prospective buyers were assured that, in time, the lots would double, triple and even quadruple in value.

Other land companies have operated similar schemes to bilk the public. Hundreds of thousands of people have received "free vacation certificates" to persuade them to attend high-pressure sales presentations at distant locations. Such "free" offers can make the consumers feel obligated to purchase property in these situations. In many cases, outright lies and misrepresentations have been used to sell worthless land. A major U.S. corporation involved in land sales was ordered to buy back all the parcels of land it had sold through flagrant misrepresentations. Afterward, the corporation, which is listed on the New York Stock Exchange, decided to abandon the land sales business.

Because of such excesses, the FTC has required at least one land company to include the following disclaimer in its contracts: "You should consider this purchase to be very risky. The future value of this land is uncertain. Do not count on an increase in its value."

Actually, to suggest that value of land "will" go up is speculative. Assertions of assured profits must be regarded as unethical conduct.

Harassment

While a licensee is expected to perform all agency duties vigorously, there is a point where zeal can turn into harassment. Repeated communications to a party who has specifically asked not to be contacted further is improper conduct, and it places the profession in a bad light.

Discrimination

A real estate licensee has a duty to understand the requirements of federal and state fair housing legislation and to practice the Golden Rule in all his or her dealings with all categories of buyers, sellers, lessors and lessees.

It is illegal and unethical for a real estate licensee to discriminate on the basis of race, national origin, color, religion, sex, physical or mental handicaps or familial status. In the course of regular business practices, it would be unethical, as well as illegal, for a licensee to take a listing if he or she was directed not to show the property to members of any of these groups. A licensee must not be a party to any transaction in which such expressed or implied exclusions are present. In addition, it would be unethical for a licensee to inquire about the ethnic or religious background of a client or customer, or to provide such information to any other party, including a principal. This should never be regarded as detrimental information that the licensee must reveal. A licensee must be fair in all of his or her dealings.

Engaging in discriminatory practices can be unethical even when apparently legal. As an example, private clubs such as country clubs often have home sites but require that all property owners belong to the club. While not excluded by the Civil Rights Act of 1866, the 1968 Fair Housing Act provided an exemption for private clubs that allow preference to members for sale or lease of housing for noncommercial purposes. If the club has de facto discriminatory membership policies based on race, religion, national origin and so on, then handling the sales of such property could put an agent in the position of appearing to support discrimination. If you placed yourself in the shoes of the groups discriminated against, this action would not pass the test of the Golden Rule.

Blockbusting

It is, of course, ethical to sell or rent property to members of minority groups despite neighborhood or community discriminatory preferences.

Blockbusting, however, is unethical and illegal. Blockbusting is a practice that induces owners to sell their homes by representing that the entrance of minority-group persons into their neighborhood will result in lower property values, higher crime or lower-quality schools. When a broker moves a minority family into an area to induce many members of the community to sell their homes, the broker is said to be blockbusting a neighborhood. While this usually is done to solicit listings, some unscrupulous licensees carry it one step further, purchasing neighboring properties at distressed prices and reselling them at inflated prices.

Blockbusting can be more subtle. As an example, a continuous practice of contacting only the nonminority members of areas for listings could be regarded as a form of blockbusting.

Steering

Steering is the illegal and unethical practice of directing persons toward or away from areas on the basis of their race or national origin.

Advertising a property in a predominantly African-American area in a newspaper primarily aimed at an African-American readership would be steering unless the broker also advertised properties in predominantly white areas in the same paper. Of course, advertising a property for sale or lease indicating racial or national origin preferences or limitations would also be steering. Using only Caucasian models in housing ads is also considered steering, as it gives readers or viewers the impression that only Caucasians are welcome.

Representing a school district as being less than desirable because of its integrated nature or forced busing program also would be considered steering. However, most steering today is more subtle. As an example, not using your best efforts to obtain an offer or lease deposit from an African-American prospect when you would try for the offer or lease deposit if the buyer were Caucasian, would be steering. It is still an illegal and unethical practice intended to maintain segregated neighborhoods or buildings.

Redlining

Redlining is the illegal lender practice of discrimination based on the racial composition of an area or perceived changes in the racial composition of an area. The name *redlining* comes from lenders who formerly marked off areas on maps in which no loans were to be made.

Redlining could consist of loan refusals, loan limitations or less desirable loan terms.

Brokers should report redlining activities to the Department of Housing and Urban Development, as well as to the state or federal lender supervising agency.

Making Things Right

In 1968, the same year that the Fair Housing Act became law, the National Association of REALTORS® added an article to its code of ethics that echoed the theme of the law. Article 10 (as amended) states:

> "REALTORS® shall not deny equal professional services to any person for reasons of race, color, religion, sex, handicap, familial status, or national origin. REALTORS® shall not be parties to any plan or agreement to discriminate against a person or persons in the basis of race, color, religion, sex, handicap, familial status, or national origin."

In 1975, the National Association of REALTORS® entered into a Voluntary Affirmative Marketing Agreement (VAMA) with the U.S. Department of Housing and Urban Development. This agreement emphasizes a voluntary affirmative program to supplement the law.

New agreement
"Partnership...."

The VAMA agreement has four basic objectives:

1. It allows REALTORS® (by voluntarily signing the agreement) to go on record as to their affirmative support of fair housing.
2. It provides for community involvement in determining fair housing problems within the community in order to formulate a plan for their resolution.
3. It provides REALTORS® with a means by which to implement their commitment to fair housing. Implementation includes education of those involved in the sale or lease of housing as to their responsibilities, developing a fair housing procedure for each firm and making certain that the firm provides equal employment opportunities by cooperating with other community groups to promote fair housing.
4. It provides for a wide range of groups to become involved in promoting fair housing. By working with the communication industries, civic organizations and groups committed to achieving the realization of fair housing, REALTORS® can take an active role in the implementation of plans to achieve the fair housing goal.

Brokers must not use their positions as members of the real estate profession to take advantage of others for personal or financial gain. In the case of disputes with their clients, licensees should willingly agree to arbitration or mediation, or both, to resolve disputes. Refusing to do so and, in turn, suing them or waiting to be sued has a detrimental effect on the profession's stature. Voluntary arbitration or mediation is an expression of good faith; a licensee should not wait until ordered by a court to pay a just claim. It is unethical to fail to pay or not offer to pay promptly a claim when the obligation is clear.

Finally, although we should choose to act ethically for ethics' sake, it's also good for business in the long run. It is a sad fact of life that some people regard the real estate profession as hopelessly unethical. And because they may believe real estate brokers to be dishonest, they often feel that they do not have to behave honestly toward brokers. All too often, people who would never consider avoiding payments to a doctor or lawyer show no qualms about trying to avoid paying a real estate broker's commission. It would be naïve to deny that this condition exists, and it exists because of the past and present excesses practiced by a small minority of licensees.

Case Study: The NIMBY Syndrome

The Foundation for Retarded Citizens announces it is in the process of purchasing a multiple-family lot in the exclusive Westwood area in order to build a 67-unit residential facility for independent living. The proposed facility conforms with local zoning regulations.

Broker Valerie Nguyen, who owns a lot next to the one that the foundation is purchasing and who also specializes in residential property in the Westwood area, is very upset by the announcement. Afraid that local property values might be adversely affected, she calls the foundation to ask whether it would consider another location. Broker Nguyen says that she knows of a good lot in a fine area across town. The foundation representative indicates the group is not interested.

Broker Nguyen then calls the lot's owner to determine whether there are any contingencies in the sale that would allow the seller to nullify the contract. She tells the seller that if he could get out of the deal, she personally will purchase the property at $10,000 more than the foundation has offered. The seller informs Nguyen that he made a contract and intends to stick to it.

Broker Nguyen calls a meeting of brokers, other businesspeople and area residents. Her opening comments are, "We must protect our homes, our families and our children. We know what will happen if these people are allowed to move into the neighborhood; our streets won't be safe. The property we work so hard for will be worthless. We must fight to protect our property." Broker Nguyen also points out that a number of the retarded would be African-Americans and Mexican-Americans.

A number of ideas are discussed at the meeting, and the group decides to go ahead with the following three proposals:

1. They will all write to the directors of the Foundation for Retarded Citizens, telling them that the organization will not be welcome in Westwood.
2. A committee will meet with the City Parks Commission to persuade them to condemn the lot for a minipark, which the group decides is badly needed in the area.
3. The group will retain an attorney to take whatever legal action is possible to delay building of the facility.

Two nights after the meeting, the office of the Foundation for Retarded Citizens is firebombed and the seller reports a telephone call in which his life was threatened if he went through with the sale.

Analysis

In our case study, broker Nguyen decided that the Foundation for Retarded Citizens should not build in Westwood. She seemed to feel that the sale of the lot to the foundation could affect her business and the value of her lot. She wasn't against the idea of the residential facility as long as it was built in someone else's neighborhood. While she didn't want the foundation to buy property in Westwood, she was perfectly willing to sell them property in another area. Broker Nguyen was practicing hypocrisy. It was acceptable for the foundation to build in someone else's neighborhood, but not in hers. This NIMBY (*not in my back yard*) philosophy fails to pass the test of the Golden Rule. She failed to consider the rights of the citizens who wished to live in the facility and the rights of the community as a whole.

Broker Nguyen appealed to people's baser attitudes in order to rally support for her cause. Her statement that property would be worthless was knowingly false and was intended to scare those in attendance. She knowingly created a panic situation in order to help prevent a worthwhile and lawful use of the land.

By pointing out that the group of residents in the facility would include African-Americans and Mexican-Americans, broker Nguyen was also appealing to racial prejudice. Writing letters to the foundation telling them that they were not welcome was probably meant to scare them. In reality, Nguyen wanted to abridge their rights to locate in Westwood.

Asking the City Parks Commission to condemn the land was tantamount to asking the city to be a part of the group's action. Hiring an attorney to delay any building was nothing more than harassment. While the specific results of firebombing and telephone threats may not have been foreseeable, they must be laid at broker Nguyen's feet. She inflamed the neighborhood by promoting fear and asked people to fight—they simply followed her advice.

Ethics Questions

1. The day before Christmas each year, broker Thomas puts on a Santa Claus suit and fills his car with gifts of candy and liquor. The gifts, which are worth between $5 and $10, are distributed to recent purchasers; owners of listings; banks, savings-and-loan and mortgage-company employees; city and county employees; local attorneys; appraisers; zoning officials and brokers and salespeople from other offices. When asked why he distributes the gifts, he replies, "It's Christmas, and I like to give gifts to others."

    What, if any, are the ethical problems of broker Thomas's behavior?

    Broker Thomas acted ethically or unethically depending upon his motive for gift-giving. Giving gifts to those you know and like is entirely proper if given in the spirit of the Christmas season. Certainly, there is nothing unethical in giving gifts to recent purchasers or to owners of property that Thomas had listed or even to other brokers.

    If gifts were given with the intent of influencing the actions of employees or agents in their jobs, which might not be in the best interest of their employers or principals, then the gift-giving could be unethical behavior. If Thomas hoped his gifts to appraisers would result in more generous appraisals, or his gifts to attorneys would result in less scrutiny of details, or his gifts to lenders would result in approval of more borderline loans or his gifts to city employees would result in relaxing rules or special treatment, then to broker Thomas the gifts would really be small bribes to influence others. In such cases, the giving of the gifts would have to be regarded as unethical conduct.

    If broker Thomas knew that an employer considered it improper conduct of his or her employees to accept gifts from firms dealing with them, then giving the gifts would be viewed as unethical conduct in that employees would be asked to breach company policy in the acceptance of gifts.

2. You are attempting to list a very expensive home. The owner tells you that he will not sell to a person of Mexican descent. You assure him that this is not a problem, as there are only a half-dozen Mexican

families in the community and they could never afford the property. Is there an ethical problem here?

Your action was unethical because in accepting the owner's discrimination, you agreed to discriminate. The listing should have been refused if the owner would not sell to a particular ethnic or racial group.

3. Normally, broker Castellano suggests that homebuyers obtain their loans through Twin Star Savings and Loan because of competitive rates and fast loan processing. Because of all the business Castellano gives to Twin Star Savings and Loan, he was asked and has accepted the offer to sit on their board of directors.

    Subsequently, Castellano becomes involved in a large land development and obtains a $10 million loan from Twin Star, the largest single loan the savings and loan has ever made. While broker Castellano abstained from voting on his loan approval, he was present when it was voted on. Based on these facts, is there an ethical problem? Would your decision be different if Twin Star Savings and Loan became insolvent after broker Castellano defaulted on the loan?

    By requesting a loan from a savings and loan of which he was a director, broker Castellano put the other directors into a situation where to refuse the loan could affect their relationship.

    Even though broker Castellano may have received no special consideration on his loan, the loan created an appearance of conflict of interest as well as insider abuse. Ethically, Castellano should not have changed hats from a director to a borrower.

    If the lender had become insolvent because of the loan it could have created public outrage, not just at broker Castellano, but toward the entire real estate profession.

4. A broker knows that a house he owns will be condemned for a development. He sells the house for $88,000 on a land contract, with nothing down and easy terms. The house has a real value of between $46,000 and $50,000. Why did the broker make this type of sale? Could the broker's action be considered ethical?

    The broker knew that at condemnation the buyer would show that he paid $88,000, which the broker hoped would result in a better condemnation settlement. Since the buyer really has no equity, whatever amount would be given in the settlement likely *would go to the broker. The broker has set up an unrealistic sale to defraud the city. He has also given the buyer the hope of home ownership without informing him that he would likely lose the property even if he made his payments.*

5. You are managing a commercial building in an ethnically mixed, stable neighborhood. One store in the building has been vacant for nine months. Previously, it was rented as a storefront church, but the tenants stayed only five months. Suddenly, three people want to rent the store: the first wants to rent the store for the regional headquarters of a white supremacy organization and offers to pay one year's rent in advance; the second wants to lease the store for Great Literature, Inc., which owns pornographic bookshops; the third wants to rent the store for a one-hour dry-cleaning plant, which would violate the local zoning ordinances. When informed of the ordinances, the dry cleaner replies, "No problem," believing that, in this neighborhood, the city would not interfere. This party also claims to have political influence. What should you do? Why?

    All three offers should be submitted to the building owner. You should explain the effect of renting to each prospective tenant on the neighborhood, as well as the likely effects of a rental on the owner's reputation in the community.

    If you personally believed that First Amendment rights should take precedence over any effect on the neighborhood, then you ethically could rent to the white supremacy group or the bookstore. However, if you believed that these groups have gone beyond First Amendment protection as to free speech and that you cannot personally be a party to such rentals, you could terminate your agency if the owner insists on renting to either of these groups.

    You cannot ethically rent to the cleaning plant for use as a cleaning plant, because you would knowingly cause a violation of the zoning ordinance. You could rent the property as a cleaning plant contingent upon obtaining a zoning variance.

6. Because a great many fires have been caused by defective wiring, a new bill proposed in the state legislature requires an electrician to certify at the time of each sale that the property's wiring is adequate and poses no immediate danger. Your broker group determines that they should oppose the legislation, for the reasons that it may slow sales, and it will cost each owner between $44 and $70 for an

inspection. Is the action of your group ethical? Why or why not? For what reason could your group ethically oppose the new legislation?

Because the bill will protect the buyers' safety and property, reasons for opposition appear to be contrary to the best interests of the public.

Your group could, however, ethically oppose the proposed law for valid reasons. For instance, if the bill failed to specify the criteria for determining "adequate" wiring and "immediate danger," this would lead to confusion. Similarly, if you felt that state building codes provided adequate protection and this inspection was simply an unnecessary redundancy created by politicians who wanted to create the appearance that they were consumer advocates, then opposition would be proper and ethical.

7. Mr. and Mrs. Wickey, a Caucasian couple, inquire about a condominium you had advertised. The Wickeys love the unit and put in an offer that the owner accepted. Before closing they ask for the return of their deposit because you failed to tell them that they would be the only Caucasian family in the six-unit building. Do you have an ethical problem?

You acted properly by treating Mr. and Mrs. Wickey in the same manner as any other prospective buyers who inquired about a property. To direct them toward properties that have primarily Caucasian tenants would be steering, which is the illegal practice of directing persons to housing based on race or national origin. Steering promotes a segregated society and must be considered unethical if the Golden Rule were to be applied, not to mention illegal.

The race of other condominium tenants should not have been disclosed, as it is not a detrimental fact of which a buyer should be made aware.

While it is unfortunate that the buyers do not want to complete the purchase, the reason is their own prejudice and was not due to any improper action on your part. Catering to the prejudices of buyers or owners who oppose integration would perpetuate segregation, which is based on different treatment of different groups. The application of the Golden Rule would require that parties be treated equally.

8. Broker Toni Swift purchased a home at a tax sale for $4,850. The house was the residence of Mr. and Mrs. Ralph Garcia, a Spanish-speaking couple. Because they do not speak or read English well, the Garcias paid what they thought were the total taxes owed on the property; in fact, they had paid only a special assessment. The Garcias did not learn of the tax sale until after the redemption period allowed by state law had expired. Broker Swift has initiated eviction procedures against the Garcias, intending to sell the property for about $80,000. What, if any, are the ethical considerations involved in this case?

   While legally right, broker Swift ethically is wrong. Her actions certainly could not stand the light of publicity or the application of the Golden Rule. She took affirmative action in order to profit from the misfortune of another. She must have realized that her actions would negatively affect the public image of the entire real estate profession.

9. Your real estate firm has just taken over the management of Cranston Towers, an older apartment complex of 420 units. Since redevelopment has upgraded the area, the owners intend to upgrade the units extensively and sell them individually as condominiums. The owners have just gotten approval for the condominium conversion and have asked you to evict the tenants so that work can be started. On November 20, you give all of the tenants 30 days' notice to vacate. Your action has been met by editorials describing you as a "Scrooge," as well as by nasty letters and phone calls not only from the public but from other licensees. What have you done wrong?

   You failed to consider the human suffering your action would cause. To start with, evictions during the Christmas season are against general public sentiment. A mass eviction such as the one you plan could have been expected to bring a great deal of negative reaction against not only your firm but the entire real estate profession. You should have attempted to obtain a delay from the owners and made a positive effort to relocate the 420 families.

10. A property manager saves eviction costs for owners by notifying the U.S. Immigration Service whenever an illegal alien becomes delinquent in rent. What are the ethical problems raised by this action, if any?

Notifying public authorities as to a violation of the law would ordinarily be commendable. In this case, the property manager is doing it, not because he or she does not want to see the law broken, but to save eviction costs. The property manager is prepared to accept illegal immigrants and profit by their occupancy as long as the rent is paid.

The property manager's action must be viewed as unethical and reprehensible even though he or she is reporting a violation. In addition, in some cases where the Immigration and Naturalization Service has been used against tenants, the tenants have used any means to pay the rent, even though they may have had to violate the law to obtain the money. The property manager has placed personal and client interests above all others. Certainly, this action would not pass the test of the Golden Rule.

11.   A disposal company wants to lease 40 acres of prime industrial property in a development area belonging to your client. They want to temporarily store toxic wastes on the site. What should you suggest to your principal?

Despite approvals and licenses, there is the real problem of leakage and land contamination, which could ruin future use of the parcel and adjoining properties. Your owner should fully understand the risks.

In the past, corporate disposal firms that leased land for storage and then went out of business were a problem. Apparently they had no intention of ever removing the stored material. Bonding disposal firms offer protection to the owners.

Even though your owner is financially protected, you have a duty to other owners. Since the area is developed, you should investigate the dangers posed to others by the storing. If there are dangers, you should recommend that the property not be leased.

12.   Thomas Closson contacts you about buying a house. Closson wants a home close to an elementary school playground or park. He tells you he enjoys watching young children. You learn that he was recently released from a state hospital for a child-molesting offense. Closson wants to put in a full-price cash offer on a home adjoining a park playground area.

You call the owners and tell them Closson wants to put in the offer. You tell them about his record, which you have verified (14 arrests and 2 convictions for child molestation). However, there are no present restrictions on Closson. You recommend to the owners that an offer not be taken from Closson but the owners say, "We need the money. Take the offer and we will accept it."

What are the problems in this case?

If you honestly believed that the rights of every individual must be protected, regardless of possible or even probable repercussions, then it would seem that you could ethically recommend to the owner that an offer be accepted. If you would sell to Closson in another neighborhood but not in an area where your own children played, then you would not be honest in any declaration that individual rights should take precedence over all other rights.

However, if we look at Albert Schweitzer's definition of ethics (See Chapter 1) that requires us to consider human society as a whole, the application of the Golden Rule to the community interests would indicate that we should take whatever legal means possible to keep Closson out of the property.

Legally, you represent the owners. Failure to take the offer could subject you to damages because of your fiduciary duty; however, you also have a duty to your community. Even though Closson may have been declared cured, his interest in a house close to a playground casts reasonable doubt on any cure. Selling the house to Closson could result in horrible repercussions.

An ethical course of action would be to return the listing to the owners, terminating your agency. But this in itself would not be enough to protect the community. At a bare minimum, the police should be notified.

While you should have immediately checked with your attorney as to your legal position, keep in mind that legal and ethical are not synonymous. You might be civilly liable to the owners if you fail to take Closson's offer, because it could breach your agency duty to use your best efforts to effectuate a sale. However, in this unusual situation, community interests should be weighed against your obligation to your principal as well as the rights of Closson. The authors believe that in this case the community interests should prevail.

5. Responsibilities to Other Licensees

Practicing the Golden Rule = Benefits for All

Duty of Professionalism

A professional is a person engaged in a calling that requires specialized knowledge, and who willingly works with others and conforms to the ethical standards of his or her vocation in order to best meet the needs of those who are served.

While striving individually for personal achievements and ethical conduct, real estate licensees also must work together to realize and maintain a high standard of professionalism within the industry. Generally, this involves little more than a healthy amount of friendly cooperation and professional respect toward other licensees. Cooperation and respect, however, do not mean that licensees should close their eyes to any unethical behavior within the profession.

Real estate licensees are highly visible within their communities. Because of the acts of a few unscrupulous licensees, the public opinion of real estate brokers and salespersons has suffered. Unless this unethical behavior is curbed by prompt and vigorous action within the real estate profession, the public's attitude will not change. If real estate licensees wish to be viewed in their communities as more than property merchants, they constantly must be aware not only of their own obligations, but of the professional obligations of all licensees.

Keeping Up-To-Date

As professionals, licensees have a responsibility to themselves and to their fellow brokers to keep up-to-date about local, state and national issues that affect the real estate business, as well as developments within the industry itself. Through their frequent meetings, seminars, courses and publications, professional organizations such as the National Association of REALTORS® and the National Association of Real Estate Brokers have helped to keep real estate licensees informed. Failing to belong to a professional organization or belonging to one and not making use of the educational opportunities afforded normally could be detrimental to those you serve unless you are taking advantage of alternative educational sources. If a licensee claims to be a professional, professional preparation must be maintained. Failing to do so is not in the public's best interest, since the licensee would not be fully prepared to properly serve the public's needs. While not the only way for real estate professionals to stay current, memberships in professional organizations can offer excellent educational sources through their various publications, meetings, conventions and special designation courses.

State mandated continuing education requirements for license renewal should be regarded as the minimum acceptable continuing education required of the licensee and not necessarily all that is needed to meet the public's best interests.

Should You Criticize Another Broker?

In general, criticizing fellow licensees has been strongly discouraged. Under normal circumstances, it is unethical to volunteer critical information concerning another licensee. If asked, you should state facts, and not opinions, concerning other members of the profession.

However, not all criticism is wrong or unethical. For example, if you firmly believe that a member of the public might be injured by dealing with a certain licensee because of the licensee's lack of integrity or ignorance, you would be remiss in your professional duty if the facts were not brought to the attention of the unsuspecting consumer. Keep in mind that if you are unable to substantiate any statement made, you could be held civilly liable for damages. Of course, generally disparaging statements, such as, "Why did you list with such a small office?" or, "He does fairly well considering his lack of experience," should be avoided, because such gossip is both unprofessional and unethical. On the other hand, if you criticized another licensee to a member of the public, but failed to do anything else about it, your actions still would be unethical. If a licensee's actions are bad enough to justify warning the public about them, they likewise should be bad enough to be reported to your state licensing authority and to any professional group with which the licensee is affiliated.

Duty To Cooperate

To fully serve a principal, the agent must cooperate with other brokers wherever possible. This means that a broker should disseminate exclusive listings as quickly as possible. The principal's interests are best served by having as many other licensees as possible work on the property to effect a quick sale. In most instances, refusing to share an exclusive listing in this manner would be unethical. Of course, a licensee would not have to share a listing if the principal requested that it not be done, but it would be unethical to suggest that such a provision be included in a listing agreement when it would not be in the principal's best interests.

In cobroker arrangements, it is unethical to fail to meet reasonable requests for information promptly or to withhold or unreasonably delay any offers received. In a listing situation in which the broker is entitled to a commission after the listing has expired, if the property is sold to a prospect who was registered with the owner before the expiration date, the broker has a duty to submit the names of prospects registered by cooperating brokers.

Although one does not have to be a real estate agent to practice appraisal (appraisers generally must obtain an appraisal certificate or license), they nevertheless are an integral part of the real estate profession. By providing appraisers with accurate data when requested, you help maintain a healthy mortgage market that can provide needed financing to allow buyer and seller agreements to be consummated. Refusing to cooperate with appraisers based on the "do your own legwork" attitude likely will result in improper comparables being used, which in the long run will work to the detriment of the real estate industry. Improper appraisals add disorder to the marketplace. They can jeopardize lenders or result in the inability of prospective buyers to become homeowners.

Some sellers' agents have been uncooperative when dealing with buyers' agents. Some refuse to split commissions or offer a lesser commission than they would to a subagent. The refusal to allow a buyer's agent to share in the sales commission amounts to a de facto refusal to cooperate. Some sellers' agents take the position that if a broker wants to be a buyer's agent, then the buyer should be paying the buyer's agent and the seller's agent can keep the entire sales commission.

Failure to cooperate with buyers' agents often stems from lack of understanding about buyer brokerage. Failing to cooperate with a buyer's agent in the same way as one would with another cooperating agent, however, works to the owner's detriment, because it discourages a buyer's agent from introducing a prospective buyer to the owner's property. Even if the buyer's agent shows the property, being solely responsible for the brokerage fee will make the property less attractive to a buyer. If an offer is made, it likely will be at a price that covers the buyer's fee obligation. The net effect of the acceptance of such an offer could be that the seller would be required to pay twice for the same services. If this refusal to cooperate is done without the seller's knowledge and approval, the seller's agent would be violating a fiduciary duty to the seller by exposing the seller to a double fee. Such action likely could lead to a court determination that the seller's agent should forfeit rights to any commission. Because an uncooperative attitude could work to the detriment of the owner, refusal to cooperate must be regarded as being unethical, as well as possibly illegal, conduct.

Avoiding Delays

If a broker is a member of a multiple listing service, it would be unethical to intentionally take the maximum amount of time allowed for listing submissions when, in fact, the listing could have been submitted earlier with reasonable diligence. Such purposeful or negligent delays work to the detriment of the principal.

Avoiding Interference with a Client

Absent a prearranged procedure or express permission to do so, contacting another licensee's client generally would be considered unethical behavior. Exceptions could, however, exist when time is of the essence and the listing broker is unavailable for consent. In such cases, the licensee's dealings with the owner should be as a representative of the listing broker. Afterward, the licensee should notify the listing broker of the situation as quickly as possible. Circumstances in which it generally would be permissible to contact another broker's principal would be to obtain information about a property or to arrange to show the property.

If a listing agent refuses to divulge the listing's expiration date or type to another agent who requests the information, then the other agent would be justified in contacting the owner. The listing agent would not be acting in the best interests of the owner by this refusal.

There can be other exceptions to general rules about direct contact with an owner who has a listing with another agent. Assume a cooperating broker, who has a subagency relationship with an owner, has an offer to purchase. The buyer refuses to extend the offer, and no one from the listing broker's office will be available until after the offer expires. If the listing agent belongs to a brokers' organization that provides procedures for contacting the owner, the procedures should be followed, if feasible. Multiple listing services generally have rules governing when an agent may contact another broker's principal. The rules might require contacting a member of the multiple listing service committee prior to the licensee taking the liberty of contacting the owner.

In a situation such as the one given, in the absence of a multiple listing procedure it would be proper to contact the owner and explain the situation, asking the owner if he or she wanted to see the offer. While such a procedure might violate the rules of your professional organization, to fail to contact the owner would be to breach the obligations to the owner owed by the subagent. A buyer's agent in a similar situation has no fiduciary duties to the owner. The buyer's agent could contact the owner to present the offer. To fail to do so in such a situation would breach the agent's duty to the buyer to see that the offer was presented. The agent should, however, strongly recommend that the owner have legal representation at the presentation.

Refusing To Cooperate with Unethical Brokers

A broker does not have to cooperate with another agent when it is not in the best interests of his or her principal to do so. As an example, if another broker has previously misrepresented properties to others, cooperating with such an agent could subject your principal to the risk of similar actions again, and thus to substantial damages. In such a case, refusing to cooperate could be ethical. However, your client should be allowed to make the determination of cooperating or not cooperating with a particular broker after you have presented the factual problems fairly. Of course, a presentation based upon your personal bias would be unethical. A license from the state does not guarantee that a person is ethical; it simply means the person has met minimum licensing requirements and has not yet acted in a way deemed sufficient to revoke or suspend his or her license.

A broker might face an ethical dilemma if he or she belonged to a professional organization that required its members to cooperate, and another member had a history of shady dealings including, say, a number of pending lawsuits involving misrepresentation. In this case, cooperating could endanger the principal. The listing broker could rightfully point out the dangers to the principal and could recommend that the principal decide against cooperating with that broker. Although such action could conceivably subject the broker to sanctions from the professional organization, it would be unethical to subject the owner to possible repercussions from allowing the unethical broker to show and sell the property based on his or her misrepresentations unless the owner knew of and accepted these risks.

Unlicensed Solicitors

Although licensees have a duty to cooperate with each other, they are not obligated to cooperate with unlicensed individuals within the industry. Even in areas of the country where it is legal, the use of paid "bird dogs"—unlicensed individuals who solicit listing and sale referrals—could be unethical, because paid bird dogs tend to go beyond just referrals. Since their pay usually is based on success, they tend to make representations about properties and what licensees can do for the buyers. Allowing owners and prospective buyers to be subject to representations by unregulated individuals generally is not in their best interests. Employing such unlicensed persons poses too great a risk of fraud to be condoned.

It is not unethical, however, to encourage friends and acquaintances to let you know about the real estate needs of their friends and acquaintances. Ethical problems arise only when they are unleashed as a pseudo-sales force working for pay.

Duty To Uphold Professional Standards

Wherever there are people and money, you will find some people trying to take unfair advantage of others. It is unfortunate that some real estate licensees have been among those unethical individuals who regard buyers as their prey.

One weakness in the real estate industry that we continue to recognize has been the hesitancy of some real estate agents to expose and condemn those agents who use fraud or unethical tactics, or both, to take advantage of buyers. Failing to promptly notify your state licensing board, as well as local district attorneys when you have reason to believe regulations or statutes are being violated must be regarded as unethical conduct. Keeping silent allows others to be taken advantage of by unscrupulous operators and reflects unfavorably on the entire real estate profession. In Florida, this ethical duty has been made a legal duty: The failure of a licensee to notify the state real estate commission about a violation of the law by another is, in itself, a violation of the law.

We cannot let the misdeeds of a few undermine the public's faith in the real estate profession. Wrongful acts to others must serve as constant reminder to us all to conduct our own affairs with the utmost integrity.

A licensee must cooperate with any governmental or professional investigation of conduct (including one's own) within the industry. Failing to do so would be unethical, as it would indicate an intent to hide an action from industry or governmental scrutiny. Since a professional is one who conforms to the ethical standards of his or her vocation, "stonewalling" also would be unprofessional conduct.

The responsibility to report the misdeeds of others applies not only to activities in other offices, but to those originating in your own office as well. There cannot be two standards of ethical conduct.

Settling Broker Disputes

Just as we expect morality in our own families, we should expect it in our professional family. Likewise, just as we have family problems at various times, we have professional problems and we should try to settle them within our professional family, rather than looking toward the courts for help. Parties to a professional dispute have a duty to make a good-faith effort to resolve their differences among themselves. In the event that they are unable to reach an agreement, the parties involved either should agree to mediation or submit to binding arbitration within their professional organization.

Lawsuits between brokers lower the image of the entire industry. In addition, customers and principals must not be inconvenienced, delayed or injured because of any broker dispute. For example, if there is a problem regarding a commission, the brokers involved should not delay a sale; this would be a disservice to both buyer and seller. In this case, a simple solution would be to hold the commission in a neutral-escrow account until a compromise or solution to the problem is found.

Professional Standards Committees

At times, ethical issues are not black and white, and brokers need help in deciding the correct course of action. Professional standards committees of local brokers' associations normally hear complaints and make decisions after the fact. Perhaps what is needed are ethics committees who try to prevent problems rather than try to deal with the problems after they have arisen. A number of state associations of REALTORS® have a legal service program that provides a legal hot line staffed daily by real estate attorneys. Unfortunately, legal advice is not necessarily ethical advice, as ethics and legality are not synonymous. An ethics hot line would help licensees help each other. The problem is being addressed by some local boards of REALTORS® by having an ethics representative to assist agents and members of the public.

Who Earned the Commission?

Although a buyer has the right to choose a broker, the buyer's wishes do not determine who has earned a commission or what is or is not ethical. Quite simply, the party who is the "procuring cause" of a sale is said to have legally earned a commission. *Black's Law Dictionary* defines procuring cause as "the proximate cause; the cause originating a series of events, which, without break in their continuity, result in the accomplishment of the prime object."

If a licensee failed to pursue a sale diligently, even after having personally initiated negotiations, his or her initial actions probably would not entitle him or her to a commission. If negotiations break down after a licensee is unable to make a sale and another licensee consummates the transaction, the first licensee would probably not be considered the procuring cause. If a broker were unable to get an offer accepted and another broker does, then the original broker could not be said to be the procuring cause.

Merely giving a buyer a property's address would not tie the buyer to a broker. It is not enough to have contributed to the sale. The chain of events leading to the sale must be without a break. To decide otherwise in the foregoing examples would, in effect, reward failure or incompetence, rather than the actual work toward successful negotiations.

Situations could exist in which a broker who, while technically not the procuring cause of a sale, nevertheless is ethically entitled to all or part of the sales commission. As an example, assume a broker has been diligently working with prospective buyers, who have expressed interest in one particular home but now want to look at other homes before making the purchase. The buyers visit the same home with another agent, but fail to mention the fact they had seen it before. The second agent convinces the buyers that this home best meets their needs and obtains an offer, which is accepted. In this case, both agents would likely consider themselves to be the procuring cause of the sale. A court might determine that one of the agents was the procuring cause and therefore is entitled to the full sales commission. However, application of the Golden Rule would indicate that both agents have some right on their side and that some apportionment of commission between them could be appropriate. In such a situation, relying on legal precedent in your state and refusing to mediate or arbitrate the matter could be unethical conduct according to the REALTORS® Code of Ethics, although it may be within the legal rights of the party.

Because determination of procuring case would be based on the particular circumstances of every case, the National Association of REALTORS® has produced the following list of 32 questions to consider in determining procuring cause. These guidelines consider the entire course of events and, while not necessarily a comprehensive list of all issues or questions, are representative of the issues and questions frequently involved in arbitration hearings.

1. What was the nature of the transaction giving rise to the arbitration request?
2. Was the property listed or subject to a management agreement?
3. Who was the listing agent?
4. What was the nature of the listing or other agreement: exclusive right to sell, exclusive agency, open or some other form of agreement?
5. Was the agreement in writing?
6. Was it in effect at the time the dispute arose?
7. Who was the cooperating broker or brokers?
8. Are all appropriate parties to the matter joined?
9. Is or was the matter the subject of litigation?
10. Were any of the parties acting as subagents? As buyer brokers? In some other capacity?
11. Did any of the cooperating brokers have an agreement, written or otherwise, to act as agent or in some other capacity on behalf of any of the parties?
12. Were any of the brokers (including the listing broker) acting as a principal in the transaction?
13. Were all disclosures mandated by law or the Code of Ethics complied with?
14. Who first introduced the ultimate purchaser or tenant to the property?
15. When was the first introduction made?
16. How was the first introduction made?
17. Did the original introduction of the purchaser or tenant to the property start an uninterrupted series of events leading to the sale (or to any other intended objective of the transaction) or was the series of events hindered or interrupted in any way?
18. If there was an interruption or break in the original series of events, how was it caused, and by whom?
19. Did the broker making the initial introduction to the property maintain contact with the purchaser or tenant or could the broker's inaction have reasonably been viewed by the buyer or tenant as the broker having withdrawn from the transaction?

20. Did the broker making the initial introduction to the property engage in conduct or fail to take some action that caused the purchaser or tenant to choose to utilize the services of another broker?
21. Was there interference in the series of events from any outside or intervening cause or party?
22. What were the brokers' relationships with respect to the seller, the purchaser, the listing broker, and any other cooperating brokers involved in the transaction?
23. What offers (if any) of cooperation and compensation were extended to cooperating brokers acting as subagents, buyer brokers, or to brokers acting in any other capacity?
24. If an offer of cooperation and compensation was made, how was it communicated?
25. If the cooperating broker(s) were subagents, was there a faithful exercise of agency on their part or was there any breach or failure to meet the duties owed to a principal?
26. If the cooperating broker(s) were buyer agents or were acting in a non-agency capacity, were their actions in accordance with the terms and conditions of the listing broker's offer of cooperation and compensation (if any)?
27. If more than one cooperating broker was involved, was either (or both) aware of the other's role in the transaction?
28. If more than one cooperating broker was involved, how and when did the second cooperating broker enter the transaction?
29. If more than one cooperating broker was involved, was the second cooperating broker aware of any prior introduction of the purchaser to the property by the listing broker or by another cooperating broker?
30. Was the entry of any cooperating broker into the transaction an intrusion into an existing relationship between the purchaser and another broker, or was it the result of abandonment or estrangement of the purchaser, or at the request of the purchaser?
31. Did the cooperating broker (or second cooperating broker) initiate a separate series of events, unrelated to and not dependent on any other broker's efforts, which led to the successful transaction?

32. Is there any other information that would assist the Hearing Panel in having a full, clear understanding of the transaction giving rise to the arbitration request or in reaching a fair and equitable resolution of the matter?

Reduced-Rate Commissions

It is unethical for brokers or broker organizations to collaborate to fix commissions. It is also illegal, as it is considered a restraint on free trade. Nevertheless, the free marketplace results in similar commissions being charged by some offices.

Some agents accept reduced-rate commissions to give themselves a competitive advantage over other agents. Lower commissions are not unethical, because they are competitive; they could, however, raise ethical problems, as addressed in Chapter 2.

Generally, an agent may refuse to work for what that agent believes to be less than fair remuneration for his or her efforts. If the agent acts as either a buyer's agent, dual agent or has told a buyer that he or she will show the buyer the property on the market that best meets the buyer's needs, however, refusing to show a lower-commission listing would breach duties to the buyer and would be unethical. Most exclusive buyer-agency contracts require the buyer to make up the difference when the buyer's agent receives less than an agreed fee.

A different problem is present when an agent refuses to cooperate with reduced-rate brokers on the agent's own listings. Unless the reduced-rate brokers have demonstrated incompetence or dishonesty, it would be in the principal's best interests to generate the greatest interest possible in the property. Depriving your principal of possible buyers to punish cut-rate brokers would be unethical. Refusal to cooperate also could be illegal, as it would be an attempt at price-fixing as well as a restraint on trade.

Referral Fees

Many real estate brokers belong to referral organizations and receive a fee from the selling agent should a referral result in a sale. Other agents individually negotiate referral fees. Some agents even advertise that they will pay referral fees.

An ethical problem arises when the prospective buyer is led to believe that the referral is solely an act of kindness to help the buyer find a home. While the prospective buyer would not be harmed by such a belief, it could be deceit. The Golden Rule would indicate that the prospective buyer deserves a full and honest disclosure as to referral relationships.

Compensating Salespeople

Brokers may pay their own salespersons and can split commissions with other brokers. A real estate broker may not directly compensate a salesperson working for another broker for any act that requires a real estate license. Any compensation to be given must be done so through that salesperson's broker. Similarly, selling bonuses offered for the sale of a property must be to the selling broker, not directly to the salesperson. The salesperson's rights to any such bonus would be based on the salesperson's contract with his or her broker. Any direct payment to the salesperson of another broker not only violates his or her contract with his or her broker, it also presents a conflict of interest, which could work to the detriment of those persons represented by the broker. In most states, it would be a violation of real estate law, as well.

Unfair Competitive Practices

Although licensees have an obligation to cooperate professionally, they also should compete vigorously with each other. Healthy competition aimed toward offering better, more professional services ultimately benefits the public and licensee alike. The following competitive practices, however, are unfair as well as unethical and must be exposed and eliminated wherever and whenever discovered:

1. Ignoring another broker's exclusive listing and approaching the owner for a listing prior to the listing's expiration, unless the listing broker refuses to disclose the type of listing and its expiration date
2. Asking an owner when an exclusive listing will expire without first asking the listing broker
3. Unwarranted pressuring or persuading of others not to do business with a particular licensee

4. Downgrading a property that has been shown to prospects by other licensees
5. Choosing a business name or logo that is similar to or could be confused with that of another area licensee
6. Agreements between brokers as to fixing fees
7. Giving information on an open listing received from a cobroker to other brokers without the cobroker's permission
8. Failing to work through a licensee who provided open listing information, unless the seller signs an exclusive listing with another broker
9. Attempting to obtain your own listing when information regarding the existing open listing was given to you by another broker, at your request, for the purpose of cooperation
10. Attempting to convert an open listing into an exclusive listing by informing other brokers voluntarily about the listing so they will have to deal through you
11. Failing to indicate, when asked for information regarding a listing, that it has expired
12. Failing to remove signs after a listing has expired
13. Placing one's own Sold sign on a property that has been listed with another office
14. Claiming to be a specialist or to otherwise have special ability when, in fact, the licensee has not had specialized training or experience
15. Removing another broker's signs from a property on which you have only an open listing
16. Failing to tell another broker that your listing is not an exclusive right-to-sell listing
17. Allowing a deal to be delayed or lost because of a commission dispute between agents
18. Refusing to arbitrate a commission dispute
19. Contacting the principal of another broker without that broker's approval or any immediate need
20. Failing to notify the local brokers' organization and state licensing agency when you become aware of an illegal act by another licensee
21. Suggesting to a principal that a listing not be distributed to other brokers when cooperating with other brokers might benefit the principal

22. Failing to supply requested information on a listing promptly
23. Delaying providing listing information to a multiple listing service by taking the maximum reporting time
24. Failing to register prospective buyers with an owner, prior to the expiration of a listing, when the prospects were registered with you by another broker
25. Directly contacting prospective buyers registered with you by another broker
26. Employing or compensating an unlicensed person for performance of acts requiring a real estate license

Case Study: When the Broker's Cooperation Is Selective

Broker Richard Schmidt of Old Town Realty owns one of the larger real estate brokerages in town, employing 16 salespeople. Schmidt has 20 years of experience in the business, including 10 years selling industrial property.

Broker Schmidt gives a 60/40 commission split to offices that are members of his multiple listing group, with 60 percent going to the selling office. When his listings are sold by an office that does not belong to the local group, Schmidt gives a 40/60 commission split, with 40 percent going to the selling office.

As a matter of practice, Old Town Realty does not cooperate with Skyland Realty, a large firm in a neighboring town. This policy stems from a bitter argument that took place three years earlier, when Old Town Realty sold one of Skyland's listings without permission. Old Town does not cooperate, either, with Kirkpatrick Realty, because Schmidt considers broker Kirkpatrick to be a shady operator who would do or say anything to get a deal through. In fact, broker Schmidt was instrumental in disaffiliating Kirkpatrick from the local brokers' organization. Schmidt also complained to the state about Kirkpatrick's actions.

Recently, broker Schmidt refused to cooperate with anyone on the sale of his own, personal apartment building that he had put up for sale with his firm. He also refused to cooperate with other area brokers in the sale of a small foundry that he listed. He did, however, send the half-million-dollar listing to several industrial brokers that he knew.

As a matter of practice, Schmidt refuses to pay any referral fees to unlicensed individuals. He is opposed to paying a commission to anyone who does not positively contribute to a sale.

A few weeks ago, Old Town Realty sent letters to property owners whose listings were about to expire. These letters began, "If you had listed with Old Town, your property would be sold by now."

Analysis

By giving them a reduced selling commission, broker Schmidt in effect discouraged brokers who do not belong to his local listing group from trying to sell his listings. This is unethical, because it is not in the sellers' best interests for listing brokers to discriminate against some brokers, thus discouraging them from seeking the sale of the principals' properties.

By not cooperating with Skyland Realty, especially for such a poor reason, broker Schmidt was again acting contrary to his principals' best interests. A principal is best served through the wide dissemination of listing information and cooperation with all qualified brokers. This really is a breach of agency duty, because broker Schmidt is not using his best efforts. This refusal to cooperate could be just cause for the cancellation of listings by owners, as it would have breached the agent's fiduciary duty. Broker Schmidt also could be liable to the owner of a property he had listed if it could be shown that this refusal to cooperate resulted in the loss of a sale.

In the case of Kirkpatrick Realty, Schmidt was trying to protect his principals by refusing to cooperate. A broker has a duty to protect the interests of his principal. A broker as well as the principal could be held liable for the fraudulent actions of a cobroker. Such actions also could reflect upon the principal's and broker's reputations. However, the decision to cooperate should be made by the principal, not by the agent.

Rather than refusing to work with Kirkpatrick Realty, a different course of action might be to refuse subagency status with Kirkpatrick Realty but agree to pay the typical subagent fee to Kirkpatrick Realty for sales where they act as buyers' agents. This course of action would increase the likelihood of a sale but keep Kirkpatrick Realty from subagency representation.

Broker Schmidt should have the owner's written consent to limit cooperation on the foundry listing. While many residential-sales specialists lack the expertise to handle an industrial sale, they nevertheless can be a source of leads. Some agents likely have knowledge and experience that would aid in such a sale. Applying the Golden Rule to the principal's interests, other agents should know of the listing and a fee arrangement worked out commensurate with contributions provided by another agent in the consummation of a sale.

A licensee should take affirmative action when the wrongdoings of another licensee become known. Broker Schmidt did this by notifying the state authorities and the local brokers' association.

Broker Schmidt's refusal to cooperate with other brokers to sell property that he owns creates an ethical problem. To espouse the principle of cooperation when dealing as an agent and then refuse to cooperate when his or her status changes to that of a principal would be hypocrisy and would not stand the test of the Golden Rule.

There is nothing unethical about a refusal to pay referral fees to unlicensed individuals. Even where legal, payment of such fees could lead to ethical problems because of the actions of these unlicensed individuals.

The letters sent by Old Town Realty were unethical. By contacting the owners before the listings expired, Old Town was not respecting the existing listings of other brokers. In addition, the language of the letter, "If you had listed with Old Town, your property would be sold by now," is a flagrant breach of ethics. Such a statement is an open criticism of the listing broker, implying a lack of the energy and expertise needed to get the job done. The letter claims that Old Town would have sold the property if it had the listing. This is a statement of opinion expressed as fact. Practices such as this cannot be condoned.

Ethics Questions

1. During negotiations, a buyer casually mentions to you that she was first shown the house for which she is negotiating a month ago, when another broker took her through it. What should you do now?

    You should ask the buyer why she did not buy from the other broker. If the other broker appears to have diligently pursued the sale, then the other agent might be the procuring cause. If there is a question in your mind as to who is the procuring cause or if the buyer simply wants to deal with you, then you should contact the other agent to explain that you will go ahead with the sale, so the interests of the buyers and sellers are not jeopardized and you will then meet with the other agent to discuss the situation.

    Even when it is clear in your mind that you are the only one entitled to the sales commission, you should contact the other agent and inform him or her of your sale. If there is any disagreement as to commission; it would not be unethical to refuse to split the commission; it could, however, be unethical to refuse to mediate or arbitrate the matter. Failure to agree to binding arbitration could be perceived as unethical conduct in that you would force the other party either to agree to a settlement in your favor or bring a costly and time-consuming lawsuit. A lawsuit concerning a broker dispute as to a commission also would reflect negatively on the real estate profession.

2. An out-of-town buyer phones in the morning, saying that he will be in town by 5 P.M. to present an offer on a property that you have listed with your firm. At 2 P.M., another broker arrives in your office with an offer on the same property. You wait for your out-of-town buyer and, when he arrives, you inform him of the details of the other offer. You then obtain his offer and present both offers to the owner. Discuss the ethics of this case.

    As soon as you received the first offer, you should have notified the owner that you had one offer and were expecting another. You should not have told your prospect the terms of the first offer, because this was unfair to both the other buyer and the other broker. You also should discuss with your client the possibility of informing the buyers that there is a competing-offer situation.

3. Broker Mary Rollins shows a house to Frank and Alan Pepper. They love the house and submit an offer on it contingent on financing. Unfortunately, they are unable to obtain financing and the deal falls through. Two weeks later, they come to your office, still looking for a house. While you're showing them several properties, they tell you about the house they'd really like to buy—the house on which they'd previously submitted the offer. You tell the Peppers that you would like to try to help them obtain financing for that property. They submit another offer on the house contingent on financing, but this time you are able to secure the required mortgage loan. Broker Rollins finds out about your actions and obtains a court order to prevent the sale from being consummated. Broker Rollins claims that she is entitled to the entire commission. Discuss the ethics of this case.

   Legally, you probably have no obligation to broker Rollins, since she abandoned the sale due to her inability to obtain financing for the buyer. Broker Rollins therefore was not the procuring cause. Your sale, however, was based partially on the efforts of broker Rollins. An ethical course of action would be to contact broker Rollins and indicate that you believe you can salvage the sale and negotiate a satisfactory arrangement as to compensation.

   Broker Rollins' obtaining a court order was unethical, because it served to inconvenience buyer and seller as well as to cast the real estate profession in a bad light. In some states, obtaining a court order to stop a transaction (an injunction) would violate state law when the purpose was to protect a claim for a commission.

4. Your longtime best friend, Stan Czernesha, visits your office to purchase a house. He tells you about an open house he just attended at Truesdown Estates, where he saw a house he wants to buy. Stan says that the salesperson at Truesdown Estates did a good selling job and encouraged him to place an offer on the spot. Stan, however, refrained from doing so because he wants you, his good buddy, to get any commission involved. What should you do, and why?

If Stan had asked you to represent him to make certain that he was protected, then you would have a duty to him and would be performing a service. You would be a buyer's agent and as such should be entitled to some compensation. However, the salesperson who actually sold Stan on the home would be ethically entitled to compensation as well. This would be a case where the parties should attempt to arrive at a mutually satisfactory commission split.

However, if you were being brought into the transaction for the sole reason for you to earn a commission, then you would be interjecting yourself into a sale by another salesperson. Since such an action could not pass the test of the Golden Rule, you should, in such a case, direct Stan back to the salesperson at Truesdown Estates.

5. One day, when your office is very busy, you tell a drop-in prospect to visit an open house being conducted by another firm. You think the house will fit her needs. However, you forget to contact the other office and fail to follow up by contacting the prospective buyer. Several weeks later, you encounter the prospect, who has in fact purchased the property. The buyer tells you that she failed to mention that you had sent her to the open house. Are you entitled to any commission split in this transaction? Why?

   You made an undisclosed referral for which you are not legally entitled to any commission. Even if you had an agreement with the other firm about referrals, your failure to tell the other office that you had sent a prospect might mean you are not legally entitled to any commission split. Even though you failed to follow good business practices, you nevertheless did contribute to the sale. An ethical approach by the selling office would be to verify the facts and provide you with some compensation for your referral as they benefited by it.

6. Broker Nellie Ortiz of Ortiz Realty obtains what she considers to be a great listing on a ranch for $467,000. Unfortunately, she can get the owner to sign only an open-listing agreement. Nevertheless, broker Ortiz makes out an information sheet on the ranch and sends it to every broker in the county as well as to many larger brokerages in nearby counties. Phil Russell, one of the brokers who receives Ortiz's information sheet, contacts the owner of the ranch and

obtains his own open-listing agreement. Russell then shows the property to a prospect, resulting in a sale on the following day. Upon hearing of the transaction, broker Ortiz asks Russell for a commission split. The local brokers' organization has named you arbitrator in this matter. How will you decide, and why?

Broker Ortiz attempted to convert an open listing to an exclusive listing by sending out unsolicited information on it to every agent in the area. If the selling broker had requested the information, he would have had a duty to deal through Ortiz, and she would have a valid claim. In this case, you should award Ortiz nothing, as her actions were improper, and Russell had no duty to deal through her.

7. At a social gathering, you are asked for your opinion of Agnes Maki by a person who is about to list a commercial property with her. You have known Maki for several years and have worked as a cobroker with her on several properties. Maki is about 65 years old and works by herself. You don't remember her ever having had a commercial listing. You tell the person, "Sure, I know Agnes—she's a nice old lady. Of course, hers is only a one-person office: I'm rather surprised that she wants to get into commercial property, because that is a little out of her field. Usually it takes a bit more energy to push commercial property. I sure hope Agnes can help you—anyway, I think she'll try." Discuss the ethics of your comments.

Your comments were unethical. You downgraded Maki by referring to her as an "old lady," giving the impression that she is senile or that her age affects her ability. The statement that she runs "only a one-person office" implies that her ability to make a sale is in question. You state that commercial property is "a little out of her field" when, in fact, you don't know what experience she has had with commercial property. Your observation that "it takes a bit more energy to push commercial property" is opinion only and implies that Maki doesn't have this energy. Because your remarks were unsubstantiated and their tone was subjectively derogatory, they were unethical.

8. You decide not to cooperate professionally with Jackson Realty, because they are not a member of any local or national professional organization, and when you sell one of their listings they take from

one to two weeks after closing to pay their cobrokers. Is your action ethical?

Your reasons for refusing to cooperate with Jackson Realty are not valid. Your position works to the detriment of owners and buyers because you are denying them the best service that is reasonably possible.

9. Broker Ron Shapiro operates a real estate service that not only takes conventional listings, but also promotes what he calls an "owner's work listing," under which he charges only a 2 percent commission. Under this arrangement, he puts For Sale signs on a property and provides some advertising, but sends all the customers directly to the owner. If any of the prospects comes to an agreement with the owner, Shapiro sends one of his salespeople over to the house to write up a sales agreement and he or she prepares everything for closing. If another broker procures a buyer for a conventional listing, Shapiro splits the commission 50/50. However, the other brokers in the area agree that Shapiro's listings should be excluded from their listing service because of his unique service, and that no members of the organization should deal with him. Based upon the facts given, what, if anything, is unethical about this situation?

This boycott of broker Shapiro is unethical. The reason for the boycott is the low commission on the "owner's work listing." Broker Shapiro is doing nothing unethical and should not be ostracized. This type of listing, or variations of it, is becoming increasingly common. These listings do not present an ethical problem as long as owners fully understand what services the broker will and will not perform.

This refusal to cooperate with Shapiro deprives principals of other agents of any sales by his agents, which would not be in their best interests.

The agreement between the brokers also could subject them to legal liability, as they likely have violated federal and possibly state laws as to price fixing and illegal restraint of trade.

10. One of your prospects tells you of her decision to buy one of the Oak Hills homes from Flash Realty. You know that a few years before, when there was an early thaw, several basements were flooded. You

reply, "Oh, that is a beautiful area! Have they solved their flood problem yet?" Was your remark proper? Why?

Your remark was improper because it gave the impression that there is a serious problem in the area, which would tend to discourage the buyer from consummating a purchase. You could have ethically pointed out that several basements had been flooded and that the buyer should find out what the present conditions are.

11. Salesperson Frank Thomas is showing a house listed with another office. Thomas finds a business card from another office on the kitchen table and leaves four of his own cards on the table next to it. Is his action proper? Why?

    This is improper because when the owner finds Thomas's cards, he or she might assume that Thomas showed the property more than once and has been working on it harder than others. If the property was not sold during the listing period, Thomas would have an unfair advantage in obtaining the listing.

12. You have an offer on a property listed by broker Singh. You go with her to present the offer. She tells you to let her do the talking, and you comply. The following transpires:
    a. Broker Singh tells the principal that the offer is really above the market value. You feel that this is not really correct, and that the offer is basically market price.
    b. She uses a comparable and quotes a sales price that is $4,000 lower than the actual sales price.
    c. Singh gives estimates of closing costs that you feel are 50 percent less than probable expenditures.
    d. She states that the small second mortgage required can easily be sold for full value, because the buyer has an outstanding credit rating. You know that the buyer's credit is fairly good, because the offer required some owner financing and you obtained credit information on the buyer. However, you doubt that the second mortgage could be sold without a substantial discount.
    What action should you take, if any? Why?

    If you say nothing, you would be as unethical as Singh, as your silence would have ratified her representation. You have a professional duty to state what you believe to be the facts before the owner signs the contract. Further, you should report Singh's actions to your local brokers' association as well as to your state licensing authority. Singh either is unscrupulous or uninformed. Either way, the unethical acts must be reported.

13. Jones Realty has an office policy designed as a listing incentive: The listing salesperson has the exclusive right to sell the new listing for 48 hours, after which other salespeople may show the property. Is the policy good? Why?

     The policy works to the detriment of the owners. Jones Realty is failing to use diligence in obtaining buyers. Diligence requires that the listing information be distributed to all salespeople and other brokers as soon as practical. The provision deprives the owner of the full service of the office for 48 hours.

14. A prospect tells a licensee that he is interested in a particular property that another broker showed him. What should the licensee do?

     First, the licensee should determine why the prospect did not buy it. Is he still dealing with that broker? If not, why not? A licensee should not thrust himself or herself into the sale of another, but if the other broker was unable to conclude the sale or was not diligent in pursuing it, or if the prospect will not deal with the other agent, then it would be proper to sell a prospect a property that was first shown by another broker. If a sale is made, the selling agent should inform the broker who first showed the property of the sale.

     The selling agent should make an effort to arrive at a settlement with the other broker if the facts warrant a settlement.

15. A Florida brokers' organization entertains a motion to censure two members for testifying in Washington, D.C., on a land fraud investigation. The members are angry because they feel the testimony reflects unfavorably on the Florida real estate profession. Discuss the ethics of this censure motion.

     The two members who testified were not guilty of fraud; they were whistle-blowers. They tried to inform the world about what was happening. Had the group censured the brokers, the censure action would have been unethical. The action of the two brokers must be commended. They showed concern for their profession, their community and the public.

16. A large investment property brokerage office has a reputation of stonewalling other agents who want information on many of their listings. Because of their reputation, other agents call them posing as prospective buyers using false identities to obtain information. Discuss the ethics of this situation.

    Failure to cooperate with other agents through delays cannot be condoned, as it works against the best interests of the property owners. What the broker likely was doing was trying to delay other agents in the hope that highly salable listings could be sold by the firm's own agents. However, the remedy of calculated deceit cannot be condoned. It is an attempt of persons to reach a proper result by unethical conduct. If the broker belonged to a professional organization, a complaint should have been made through that organization or other brokers should have personally tried to resolve the stonewalling problem. The British real estate trade group, The National Association of Real Estate Agents, specifically forbids this type of activity: "A member shall not contact another agent posing as an applicant . . . ."

17. The activity of Broker Lutz is devoted almost entirely to buying property for personal and family investment purposes. Lutz calls Borowski Realty and salesperson Shahidi shows broker Lutz a large apartment complex that his firm recently had listed for sale. After viewing the property and at his request receiving extensive data prepared by salesperson Shahidi, Lutz finally reveals his status as a broker by saying, "I will be preparing an offer through my brokerage office as selling broker." Discuss the ethics of this situation.

    Broker Lutz's failure to reveal agency status with a secret intention of depriving salesperson Shahidi of a sales commission was deceit and must be regarded as being unethical. Apparently broker Lutz wanted the benefits of being a broker to cut his purchase costs, but he wanted other agents to do his work for him.

Borowski Realty could properly refuse to pay a co-op fee or allow subagency for broker Lutz. However, the facts of the situation and the refusal to cooperate should be revealed to the owner of the listed property and any offer received would have to be presented to the owner.

6. Responsibilities to Other Licensees within Your Office

Fairness to Coworkers = Positive Working Environment

Hiring Practices

Ethical dealings with the people in your office must begin when they join the firm. When hiring salespeople, it would be unethical for a broker to make false or misleading statements implying that salespeople are earning more money than they are. It would be unethical to advertise for or otherwise obtain salespeople by subterfuge. For example, advertising for salespeople under a different job heading in the classified section of a newspaper, or giving the impression that the job pays on a salaried basis, when in fact it is commission only, is deceptive.

Discriminatory hiring practices are unethical as well as illegal. Again, it is illegal and unethical to discriminate based on sex, race, religion, national origin, age, handicap or familial status; as is asking questions to determine any of these characteristics during the interview process. For example, you may not ask an applicant, "Where were you born?" to determine whether he or she is a citizen; you may, however, ask, "Are you legally able to work in the United States?"

In many cases, members of minority groups often do not apply for certain jobs because they believe they will not be hired by firms that do not have minority salespersons on staff. While failure to actively recruit minority group members as salespeople would not necessarily be unethical, it would be ethical and an affirmative action to do so. By letting persons from minority groups know that the profession is open to them, every broker can play a part in helping to end segregated offices. Such action will reflect positively upon the real estate professions.

It could be unethical as well as illegal to set minimum hiring requirements that do not relate to the function of the position. Setting qualifications greater than what the job requires could be discriminatory. You should, therefore, give careful thought to any personnel test or minimum formal educational requirements.

If a broker is also a REALTOR®, then signing the VAMA (Voluntary Affirmative Marketing Agreement), discussed in Chapter 4, would be a positive step toward showing your commitment both to fair housing and to aiding minorities in entering our profession.

Another positive step is seen in the example of a California broker who has her own program for minority interns. The students attend a real estate licensing school one day per week, have weekly counseling sessions with the broker and attend various office meetings as part of their training.

The Americans with Disabilities Act exempts employers with fewer than 15 employees from the requirement to make reasonable accommodations in the workplace to meet the needs of handicapped employees. Therefore, such firms could legally discriminate in the hiring of handicapped individuals. However, it would be unethical for any firm, including a real estate office, with fewer than 15 employees to deprive an otherwise qualified person from a job when reasonable modification of the premises would allow that person to work for you. Examples of such modifications might be wider aisles between desks to accommodate a wheelchair, a new desk to accommodate a wheelchair, grab bars in the washrooms, a paper-cup dispenser by the water fountain, reasonable ramping of steps, special handicapped parking space for the employee and so on.

The broker should investigate the ethical character of an employee or associate during the hiring process; the mere fact that the state has issued someone a salesperson's license is no guarantee that the person is ethical. Remember, the broker is allowing a salesperson to represent the firm and its clients as well as to act in a fiduciary manner. When a prospective salesperson has previously worked for other brokers, the hiring broker should check with the former broker(s) as to the character of the salesperson. The unethical acts of one agent could reflect on the other salespeople as well as the broker. In some states, a broker's failure to properly investigate a salesperson's background could result in suspension or revocation of the broker's license.

Employee Contracts

A broker should have a written, signed contract with every employee, outlining all obligations and duties of both broker and salesperson. A contract will prevent many disputes caused by misunderstandings between broker and salesperson. A broker-salesperson contract should address such issues as commission splits, draws, employee benefits, use of phone and postage, correspondence procedures, rotation of calls and walk-ins, rights to listings and sales in progress after termination of employment and so forth. The broker should ensure that the salesperson fully understands the terms of the contract before signing it.

In most cases, broker-salesperson contracts are independent contractor agreements that set forth the duties and responsibilities of the parties. A principal reason why an independent contractor agreement is used is that it is required in order to relieve the broker, under IRS rules, from a duty to make Social Security contributions or to withhold federal income taxes from commissions earned. Despite the independent contractor agreement of the parties, most states treat broker-salesperson relationships as employer-employee relationships as to broker responsibility for acts of salespersons.

Part-Time Brokers and Salespeople

A part-time broker generally should refrain from employing salespeople, because a broker who is frequently unavailable due to other interests cannot adequately supervise a staff. In at least one state, this practice is illegal. By the same token, it could be unethical for a broker to hire part-time salespeople for normal real estate brokerage. A part-time salesperson's time may be greatly restricted, and this employee may have trouble following up leads and may be unable to properly meet the needs of clients and prospective buyers. Of course, if the part-time salesperson was able to properly meet the needs of buyers or sellers, then there would not be an ethical problem.

Some brokers have solved ethical problems associated with using part-time salespersons by pairing part-time salespeople with full-time associates. A fee-sharing arrangement is made for the supervisory salesperson who is available to meet the needs of buyers and sellers when the part-time salesperson is not available.

Many salespeople employ real estate licensees on a part-time or full-time basis as assistants. They can staff open houses, handle phone solicitations, set up appointments as well as handle many other time-consuming tasks, which frees the salespeople (employers) for more productive work.

Providing opportunities for part-time salespeople allows them to learn the real estate business without giving up other jobs. This increases the likelihood of their success if they go to work full-time at a later date. It can also be a positive action in helping minority group members to enter the real estate profession.

Assistants

Real estate salespeople (or brokers) who employ assistants should have a written contract with the assistants that clearly spells out duties, salary and benefits. The parties should ethically agree to arbitrate any dispute that may arise out of the employment. This will avoid possible lawsuits that could have a negative affect on the reputation of the employing salesperson, the firm and the entire real estate profession.

Real estate professionals who employ assistants have a duty to supervise them. In cases of unlicensed assistants, the employing salesperson must make certain that the assistant does not perform any act for which a real estate license is required. It would be illegal and unethical for a real estate licensee to state, or otherwise allow others to believe, that an unlicensed assistant was either licensed or capable of performing duties which require a real estate license.

Many states are seriously considering regulations to address the use of unlicensed assistants.

Overstaffing

Often brokers will hire every salesperson they can get, even though the office is not generating enough business for the present sales staff. This overstaffing practice, which does not aid the public, works to the detriment of the salespeople. Overstaffing could actually work to the detriment of the public, because it sometimes results in overly competitive or questionable practices among the licensees. Overstaffing could therefore be considered unethical. Because of higher "desk cost" associated with each salesperson, overstaffing is not as common a practice today as it once was.

Setting Fair Policies

If brokers are ethical in their dealings with the other brokers as well as with salespeople within their own office, they can reasonably expect that their salespeople also will act in an ethical manner. Thus, the broker sets the ethical climate for the office. The broker should set forth a series of clearly defined office policies and make sure that they are strictly followed. These policies must be fair to the general public as well as to the other licensees in the firm. The broker must ensure that the office policies are fully understood by all concerned—it must be clear that the object of the rules is fair play for all. Needless to say, it would be generally unethical for either the broker, an employee or associate not to respect an established office procedure.

Duty To Supervise

Since real estate salespersons are licensed under a real estate broker, the broker has a duty to supervise for his or her salespersons. Failing to properly supervise employees or associates is unethical and is a violation of state licensing laws as well. In any dispute in which a salesperson is involved, it is no excuse for a broker to claim ignorance of what the salesperson was doing—it is the broker's duty to know. The duty of supervision exists regardless of whether the salesperson is technically considered an employee or independent contractor since, to the public, the salesperson represents the broker.

Today, we have many 100-percent-commission offices where salespersons essentially rent office space and a broker's name by paying fees to the broker for their desk and office services. There is nothing unethical about 100-percent-commission arrangements. The broker, however, should not feel that there are no longer any supervisory duties. To be licensed as a broker generally requires greater knowledge, experience and/or education than is required of a salesperson. It would be a disservice to the public to allow a salesperson to act as a broker without supervision. Therefore, the broker should review listings and sales agreements of these salespersons and treat them as any other broker would as to questionable, illegal or unethical conduct.

Real estate brokers often hire untrained salespeople and put them in sink-or-swim situations without the benefit of the basic training required for survival. A broker who cannot or will not train or provide training opportunities for new salespeople should not hire untrained salespeople. Doing so would not be fair to the salespeople because it reduces their chances of success—and this would have to be considered unethical conduct.

Respecting Other Licensees' Rights

When a licensee brings a prospective buyer or seller into the office, other licensees should not interfere with any sales presentation or otherwise attempt to influence the prospective buyer or seller. If one licensee has failed to follow up on a prospect, another may intercede, but the second licensee should first notify the first licensee of this intention.

It could be unethical for a licensee to indicate that an offer had been received or accepted when the offer was not in writing. Likewise, it would be improper for any licensee to fail to bring a listing he or she had received into the office within a reasonable length of time which would customarily be the next business day at the latest.

In the event that a salesperson is contacted by a prospective buyer who had already been dealing with another salesperson in the office, he or she should suggest that the prospect contact the first salesperson. The second salesperson in this situation may show a property to the prospect only if the prospect does not want to deal with the other licensee or if the other licensee is unavailable for a time. In any event, the original licensee must be notified if another salesperson is dealing with his or her prospect. It would be proper in such a case to negotiate an equitable commission split if the efforts of the first salesperson contributed to the sale of property.

Commissions

A broker should handle all salesperson commissions equitably. If a broker agrees to different commission rates for different salespeople, it could foster discontent and could be unfair. However, it would be fair and equitable to give greater commissions to salespersons who had been with the firm for a longer period, providing this time differential was offered to all salespersons. Similarly, sliding-commission scales are proper with higher commission given to salespersons who achieve a greater volume, providing that the sliding scale applies to all salespeople. Such a sliding commission encourages salespeople to exert greater effort for their success. If a salesperson personally handles financing for buyers or handles work normally performed by the broker, then an increased commission might be justified. However, the same opportunity should be made available to other salespeople who are capable of handling the same tasks. A broker should pay commissions as soon as is practical after a sale is consummated; failing to do so could be unethical based on the application of the Golden Rule. If a broker grants a salesperson a draw against a commission, the draw must be from the broker's own personal funds, not from any funds held in trust.

Clarifying Roles

If a person licensed as a broker or salesperson works for an office in the capacity of a salesperson, he or she should not maintain or work for a separate office or engage in real estate activities unless done through the employing broker. A broker working as a salesperson may not have a separate trust account. Trust monies must be kept in his or her employing broker's trust account. Working as both a salesperson and broker or as a salesperson for more than one firm likely would result in conflicts of interest as well as confusion by the public about that person's role. This practice is, in fact, illegal in most states.

If a broker rents desk space from or shares an office with another broker, both brokers must inform the public, through use of different business signs or other such identification, that they are separate, nonrelated brokers.

When a licensee purchases property or sells his or her own property listed for sale with his or her office, the supervising broker must ensure that this fact is disclosed to all parties involved, that the property was listed at a fair price and that the seller's interests are fully protected or that the buyer was treated fairly with full disclosures.

Reprimanding Employees

While a broker should support his or her salespersons when he or she believes that their actions were proper, the broker must take appropriate measures to rectify wrongful acts and to ensure that they will not be repeated.

A pitfall that occasionally traps some brokers is failing to properly reprimand an employee or associate, who is a friend, for unethical behavior. Some brokers find it particularly difficult to reprimand a salesperson when the unethical acts result in a successful transaction. Other brokers neglect to reprimand their employees harshly enough because they are afraid that their salespeople, particularly the "good producers" in the office, will quit and go elsewhere. As we have already said with regard to licensees in other offices, failing to properly reprimand a licensee for unethical behavior amounts to approving the behavior.

Employee reprimands should be based on the severity of that person's improper actions. If a licensee is guilty of acts that cast serious doubt on his or her character, the licensee should be discharged. Likewise, if the licensee continues a course of unethical behavior after a reprimand, the licensee should be discharged. In any case, the broker should fully investigate all aspects of the situation and determine whether the licensee's behavior was, in fact, unethical. Remember, it is unwise for a broker to keep an employee on the staff when there is reason to believe that principals, customers or the general public will be subjected to the actions of a person who does not exhibit the high behavioral qualities expected of a licensee. Likewise, it could be poor practice for a salesperson to remain with an office after ascertaining that the supervising broker either is guilty of, or condones, unethical behavior.

The Dangers of Dollar Worship

In some real estate offices, sales or listing volume is the only achievement given special recognition. This sole emphasis on earnings can negatively affect the professionalism most real estate salespeople are striving for. Emphasizing only dollars earned could seemingly justify questionable though successful conduct. It would, therefore, be beneficial conduct for a broker to honor the professional and educational achievements of his or her salespersons as well as meeting the needs of buyers and sellers.

In one bleak view of the effects of the emphasis on financial success, a former regional training director for a major land developer stated:

> "Demanding high-volume sales regardless of how they are made weeds out all honest and sincere men . . . and you wind up with only the hard core who would sell their own mother down the river for a buck . . . ."

Although this attitude is not prevalent among general real estate brokers, it has in the past represented the attitudes of some large land developers. Supervision often has been result-oriented, with little regard for the means employed to gain the results. In many cases, salespeople were actually taught illegal and dishonest sales presentations.

When faced with charges of wrongdoing, the land companies usually claimed that they themselves were pure, but they had problems with greedy salespeople who made false claims and were deceptive in order to obtain greater commissions. They said they fired these people whenever they discovered any wrongdoing. In all too many cases, the courts have found that salespeople were encouraged and even trained in deceptive sales tactics. It was not a case of just a few "bad apples." While far removed most from normal brokerage, the land project salespeople are nevertheless licensees. Their excesses can never be condoned, and their actions reflect on the reputation of every licensee.

To emphasize professionalism rather than just dollars, some offices pick up all or part of tuition costs for special professional courses, and in some cases college courses. Other offices provide special commission splits to salespersons who have achieved particular professional designations. This commission differentiation is proper if it is available to all of the firm's salespeople. It can serve as an excellent incentive for salespersons to become better qualified to meet buyer and seller needs.

Reporting Unethical Acts

If a licensee violates real estate laws, it is the supervising broker's duty to report the licensee's actions to the state real estate licensing agency, local district attorney or local professional association, as applicable.

Similarly, if a salesperson finds that his or her broker's actions are in violation of real estate laws, then the salesperson has an ethical duty to report the broker's activities to the proper authorities. In at least one state, failure to report a known violation would subject a licensee to disciplinary action.

Settling Disputes

In the event of any interoffice dispute, both brokers and salespeople have a duty to resolve disagreements by negotiation, mediation or arbitration rather than by litigation. Refusing to mediate or arbitrate office disputes could be unethical. As previously stated, lawsuits between real estate agents tend to lower the image of the entire real estate profession and have a negative effect on the working relationships within the office besides wasting time and money.

Terminating Employees

When a broker or salesperson's employment is terminated, it would be unethical for the supervising broker to make false or misleading statements to prevent the licensee from obtaining another position. On the other hand, if the broker knows of a past employee's serious unethical actions, the broker should consider notifying this person's future employer in order to protect that broker's clients and customers. Such notification should be limited to facts that can be proven and should not include suspicions or opinions.

Case Study: Different "Strokes" for Different Salespeople

Broker Joan Cotter of Big Town Realty is facing two important personnel decisions.

Two of her top salespeople are considering leaving her firm to join Greenland Realty on the other side of town. They approach Cotter and tell her they will stay on with Big Town only if she matches the commission split that Greenland Realty is offering its salespeople. They give Cotter three days to make a decision. After discussing the matter with her accountant, Cotter concludes that she cannot match the Greenland Realty commission split. Instead, she decides to offer these two salespeople a 100-percent-commission plan. Under the proposed plan, they will receive 100 percent of the commissions paid on deals they negotiate, without having to split with their supervising broker. Each will be required to pay Big Town Realty $500 per month plus a $200 transaction fee. In return for fees, these salespeople will receive office space, secretarial support and broker assistance. Cotter will still be responsible for supervising the two salespersons. Cotter is certain that these two salespeople will go for her proposal.

The other problem facing Cotter is what to do with salesperson Marilyn Gottleib. Of all her salespeople, Gottleib requires the most supervision—she always seems to need help. Even after two years on the job full time, Gottleib is not really making a living. In fact, she has made only three sales and has taken only four listings in the past year. Broker Cotter has considered firing her for some time, feeling that she is taking up valuable desk space while not contributing her share to the office income. This morning, Gottleib brought in a 10 percent exclusive-right-to-sell listing on a choice 400-lot subdivision. One of Cotter's salespeople is already negotiating with a builder who has said he wants to purchase all 400 lots. Gottleib has a contract with Big Town Realty specifically stating she has no rights to any listing commissions after she leaves the firm. Cotter decides to terminate Gottleib's association with the firm tomorrow morning.

Analysis

The 100-percent-commission plan is not unethical, but by offering a 100-percent-commission plan to only two of her salespeople, Joan

Cotter is not being fair to the rest of her staff. While Cotter could place a reasonable criteria for salespersons being offered the 100-percent-commission plan, it should be available to all qualified salespersons.

A second, more complex problem exists in broker Cotter's actions toward Marilyn Gottleib. Gottleib apparently has not proven herself to be a satisfactory salesperson. Although Cotter has the right to sever their relationship, the reason that has triggered the action at this time appears to be to deprive Marilyn of her listing commission. Terminating her for this reason would clearly be unethical and also would probably have a detrimental effect on office morale.

A more subtle problem is that of handling listing commissions when sales are made after a salesperson leaves a broker. There is no question that the listing is the property of the broker and that it stays with the broker's office when a salesperson departs. The question is whether the salesperson should have any right to commissions earned by virtue of that salesperson's listing when the property is later sold. Such matters normally are set forth in a salesperson's contract; some brokers pay the commission, while others do not. Some brokers execute a termination agreement with salespersons that spell out the rights and obligations after termination of employment. By applying the Golden Rule to such a situation, it would seem that if a licensee contributed valuable effort toward a sale, then that licensee should share in the reward. It should make no difference that the licensee is no longer with the broker for whom the property was listed. To decide otherwise would be to unjustly enrich the broker, who would not have to share the commission with a licensee who contributed to the successful sale. However, the listing licensee would not be ethically entitled to any commissions for listings after they expire.

It must be understood that a listing commission isn't paid solely for the act of obtaining a listing. The listing salesperson is expected to service the listing by performing such duties as keeping the owner informed and advising the owner on ways to make the property more desirable. If a salesperson leaves a broker, the obligations of the listing salesperson could not be fulfilled. A reduced listing commission in these cases would therefore appear equitable and should be spelled out in the salesperson's contract with the broker or in a termination agreement.

There is a correlation between high morale and high production. As a result, a healthy and fair attitude exhibited by both broker and salespeople can help achieve a healthy business.

Ethics Questions

1. Amy Mauck, who was disfigured in a fire and has recently obtained a real estate license, answers your ad for "Real Estate Salespersons Wanted." Your ad indicated you would provide training. You complete your normal interview and tell her that the successful candidates will be contacted within one week. You do not intend to contact her, as you feel her appearance will make buyers and sellers uncomfortable. Is there an ethical problem?

    You are discriminating against Mauck because of her appearance. Your mindset, if adopted by others, would result in her being unable to work in any situation where she would have contact with others. Put yourself in her place—wouldn't you want a chance to prove yourself? This action clearly fails the test of the Golden Rule and must be regarded as being unethical. This discrimination against Mauck is not much different than discriminating against people because they are fat, have accents and so on. All such discrimination is wrong and should not be condoned even if it is not specifically prohibited by civil rights laws. Always consider the Golden Rule. In this particular case, you might also be in violation of the Americans with Disabilities Act.

2. You are a broker. Your salesperson, Bill Franco, shows prospect Elaine Collins a house. A week later, Collins enters the office and asks to see the same home. Salesperson Ralph Johnson shows the house and makes the sale. The prospect never mentions that she had seen the property with salesperson Franco. Both salespeople claim they are entitled to the commission. What should you do?

    Often, buyers fail to consider the implications of dealing with multiple salespeople. Salesperson Franco, by making the first showing, instigated the action that led to salesperson Johnson's consummating the sale. Each acted in good faith and contributed to the final sale.

    You should explain the situation to the two salespeople and suggest that they work out an agreeable commission split. If they are unable or unwilling, you should then suggest mediation. If mediation fails to resolve the problem, you should then suggest that you arbitrate the dispute. In many offices, mediation and binding arbitration by the broker are agreed to in the contract the salespeople sign.

Keep in mind that while you should strive for an agreement between the salespersons, the final determination is your responsibility as the broker.

3. Mojave Spa Brokers and Developers advertises for salespeople, offering free license training. However, they charge $75 for the textbook, which was not mentioned in the ad. The license training included learning sales presentations on "Beautiful Mojave Spa." After three sessions, all trainees are told they have to visit Mojave Spa in order to continue the course, and a bus trip is arranged. A reception is held at the site, and free food and liquor are provided. A number of salespeople are present; they impress the trainees with how much money they are making with the firm. Then, for the first time, the trainees are given an opportunity to buy a lot with no down payment and at half-price if they sign up that day. They are told that they really can't expect to be successful unless they have faith in the project and that it will impress customers to know that the salespeople have purchased lots. Discuss the ethics of the case.

    Mojave Spa's actions are, of course, unethical. In their ads, they should have specified all costs and obligations. The salespeople were apparently recruited under false pretenses. The Mojave Spa was interested in recruiting customers, not salespeople.

    The presentation at Mojave Spa appealed to the greed factor emphasizing making big money in sales, and also of a special bargain with the half-price lot.

4. Swenson Realty employs 38 salespeople, all women 40 years old or older. No male salespeople are employed. The broker, Inge Swenson, says she doesn't hire men because she finds that after a while they resent working for a woman. She wants older women because she feels younger women lack the credibility necessary for success in real estate. Does Ms. Swenson have an ethics problem? What is it?

    Ms. Swenson does have an ethics problem—she discriminates on the bases of age and sex in her hiring practices and has likely violated state as well as federal equal employment opportunity acts.

5. DelaCruz Realty is selling the Far Away Heights subdivision, which includes nine model homes open on Saturday and Sunday afternoons. DelaCruz hires part-time licensed salespeople who work weekends only, taking orders on prefilled-out forms and receiving $250 for each sale completed. These salespeople do not come to the office. DelaCruz visits the site frequently and has designated one of the salespeople who has had prior extensive real estate experience as a project sales manager. The project sales manager regularly consults with DelaCruz. Is there any ethical problem here? If so, what is it?

    There is no ethical problem here. The part-time salespeople are able to adequately meet the needs of the customers and owners and apparently have adequate supervision.

6. Salesman Eng is one of your real estate salespeople. He is involved in an auto accident while showing property. Apparently, while pointing out a house, he failed to observe another car. Both Eng and his two prospects are seriously injured. You discover that Eng has no insurance—as a matter of fact, his auto insurance was canceled two years ago because of his driving record. What are the ethical and legal problems involved here?

    You failed in your duty to adequately check the background of your salespeople. Because they would be taking prospects in their cars, you had a duty to ascertain that appropriate insurance coverage was in place and was maintained. In this case, your failure to do so worked to the detriment of prospective buyers. You have also exposed yourself to liability claims.

7. ABC Realty received a listing on a four-bedroom colonial in the prestigious Shoreland area. All the salespeople in the office immediately started calling their sales prospects, because they all thought this listing would sell in a matter of only a day or two. Ms. Elliot, a salesperson for the firm, showed the property to Mr. and Mrs. Lorenzo, who loved the house and felt the price was fair. Mr. Lorenzo told Ms. Elliot that he would first like all of them to go to his attorney's office, because he wanted the attorney to examine the written offer before he signed. On the way to the attorney's office, Ms. Elliot stopped and called her office. She told the broker, "I've sold the Shoreland home. I will be in shortly with the full-price offer."

The attorney, Matthew Broadstreet, told the Lorenzos that most asking prices are more than people really expect to receive. He recommended an offer $10,000 below the asking price of $230,000. Ms. Elliot tried to raise the offer, but attorney Broadstreet prevailed. She brought in the $220,000 offer. What are the ethical considerations of this case?

Ms. Elliot should not have said the property was sold before she possessed a contract and deposit that had been signed by the buyers and accepted by the sellers. She was attempting to discourage others from showing the property in order to avoid multiple offers.

8. You learn that Bill Cohn, an 83-year-old broker, who currently resides in a nursing home, employs Tessie Clyde as a salesperson. Ms. Clyde handles every transaction completely, but pays Cohn $100 from every sale made. Is there an ethical problem here?

Broker Cohn is apparently not supervising Ms. Clyde, and this could work to the detriment of the public. For all practical purposes, Ms. Clyde is working as a broker, although she apparently lacks the qualifications or she would be one. You should report both broker Cohn and Ms. Clyde to the appropriate authorities.

9. Unfortunately, some brokers encourage or condone the unethical and illegal activities of their salespeople when they are successful. What are some possible solutions?

In the past, penalties have been light and in many instances nonexistent. Often brokers and developers have avoided punishment by signing consent agreements in which they don't admit any wrongdoing but promise not to do the particular act in the future.

If state departments of real estate and attorneys general would work together to ensure swift and severe punishment for wrongdoing, the number of fraudulent actions likely would be reduced. In addition, if brokers were held more strictly liable for the actions of their salespeople this would encourage more vigilant supervision.

Individual real estate agents and real estate organizations should increase their vigilance as to what is happening in their profession and take an active role in reporting and discouraging even the hint of impropriety. All brokers must receive the message that the industry will not condone illegal or unethical behavior of a few since it reflects on all.

10. There is an extremely high turnover rate among new licensees. What are some of the likely reasons for this?

    Brokers often fail to properly counsel prospective employees during the interviewing process. In the desire to hire more sales-people, they sometimes fail to discuss the problems encountered by new salespeople and the qualities required for success.

    Brokers often hire untrained salespeople and put them in a sink-or-swim position without providing them with the basic train-ing necessary to survive. Some brokers are busy making sales and don't provide support for their salespeople when needed. Brokers who cannot or will not provide training opportunities for sales-people should not hire untrained people, because it is a breach of an implied duty to provide training and assistance, and in some states it would be a violation of state license law or regulations.

    Some brokers advertise unrealistic earnings and new licens-ees become disillusioned when they find out what the other sales-people are actually making.

    Some salespeople are attracted to real estate by the "fast buck" image and when they find that success involves hard work, they leave.

11. It is alleged in a lawsuit by a salesperson that a broker who special-ized in investment properties penalized agents who brought in offers above the list price by denying such agents any commissions for the sales. If true, what was the likely reason for this policy? What are the ethical considerations involved?

    The broker may have wished to avoid bidding situations. In this case, the broker also stated that he felt offers above listing price were inflationary and should be discouraged. The broker did not understand his fiduciary duty to his principals, the sellers, which should have taken precedence over personal feelings. Offers above list price would definitely be in a seller's best interest, as would competitive bidding situations. To discourage these offers in this manner deprived the principals of dollars which the market indi-

cated buyers would pay. By punishing the salespeople, the broker was able personally to receive greater profit for offers above the sales price while denying compensation to the sales agents. On the other hand, the sales agents by taking offers above list price were best meeting the interests of their principals, but were punished for it. The broker's actions cannot pass the test of the Golden Rule when applied to the principals as well as to his salespersons.

12. Broker Elman has his receptionist transfer all inquiries from callers having Spanish surnames or who appear to be Mexican-American to Rose Garcia. Rose Garcia is his only Mexican-American salesperson, although several other salespeople in the office can speak Spanish.

　　All other callers are divided among the other nine agents in the office. Does broker Elman have an ethics problem?

Apparently, broker Elman feels that Mexican-Americans will be more comfortable dealing with a Mexican-American or that a Mexican-American is more likely to sell a Mexican-American a home. In either case, broker Elman has failed to consider other salespersons in the office as well as the callers and Rose Garcia.

Application of the Golden Rule as to other salespeople could reveal that his actions are unfair in that to give all of these calls to Rose Garcia deprives other salespeople of a chance to make a sale. Rose Garcia has been cast by the broker as a Mexican-American sales agent and not just a sales agent.

7. Broker Trust Funds

Discretion + Careful Record-Keeping = Secured Funds

In the real estate profession, the term *trust funds* refers to money or things of value received by a broker or a salesperson in the course of a transaction or duties that do not belong to the broker or salesperson but are being held for the benefit of others.

Earnest Money

To show that a buyer is acting in good faith, most offers to purchase real estate are accompanied by a deposit known as *earnest money*. Purchase agreements frequently provide for the forfeiture of the buyer's deposit as the measure of damages should the buyer default on the purchase agreement. In the absence of such a provision, the seller could sue for actual damages that could exceed the amount of the earnest money deposit or, in some states, sue for specific performance.

If a buyer's offer is rejected, the broker must return the earnest money deposit to the buyer in a prompt manner. Failure to return the deposit in a prompt manner would be unethical behavior, as it could not pass the test of the Golden Rule and may also violate state license law.

In taking a deposit, the broker is doing so for a specific purpose. The broker has no rights to the deposit. Therefore, it would be unethical and generally illegal for a broker to keep any portion of a deposit based on a separate claim that the broker has against the buyer. As an example, assume that the broker has a claim against the buyer based on a separate transaction. If the buyer's offer is not accepted, the broker should not use the buyer's deposit to offset against what was due the broker. The entire deposit must be returned.

As a seller's agent, you would want to obtain as large a security deposit as possible. The larger the deposit, the less likely the buyer is to change his or her mind about completing the purchase and intentionally defaulting on the purchase agreement. With a small deposit, the buyer is more likely to walk away from the purchase, especially if the purchase contract provides that the seller's sole remedy in the event of buyer default would be the forfeiture of the earnest money deposit.

Buyer offers sometimes provide for a relatively small earnest money deposit, a long period prior to closing and a provision that forfeiture of the deposit shall be the seller's sole remedy in the event of buyer default. From a seller's point of view, such an offer is equivalent to an option to buy and the earnest money is really the option price. Sellers' agents should make certain that sellers fully understand such agreements.

Buyers' agents may suggest large earnest money deposits when the offer is less than full price in order to convince a seller to accept an offer that might otherwise have been rejected. Earnest money is not required to have a binding contract, but sellers are justifiably wary of buyers who refuse to make deposits of good faith with their offers.

Earnest money need not be money. It can be a promissory note or even personal property. However, if other than cash, the seller must be informed of the nature of the earnest money deposit so that any decision made is based on a complete understanding of the agreement.

When a broker receives a deposit, either for a purchase or a rental, he or she is acting in the role of a stakeholder, holding the deposit for others. When handling funds or property of others the broker has a duty to act in a responsible manner. Failure to take reasonable steps to protect these funds would have to be regarded as unethical behavior, since it would be contrary to the interests of the parties having rights to the funds.

Failing to reasonably protect deposits also would be a violation of a broker's fiduciary duty.

If a purchase offer provides for it, some states allow earnest money deposits to be turned over to the seller. An agent, in obtaining an offer, should not suggest such an arrangement without the buyer understanding that his or her deposit could be in jeopardy should the seller be unable to complete the sale and be unable or unwilling to return the deposit. The ethical course of action would be to explain the other alternatives offering greater protection to the buyer.

The same holds true for purchase agreements that provide for all or part of the purchase funds to be turned over to the seller prior to transfer of title. Should the seller be unable or unwilling to transfer a marketable title, the buyer would be in a position of trying to regain his or her funds. Failure to inform the buyer fully of possible problems in such a situation would be unethical behavior on the part of the selling agent.

The earnest money check could be made out to the trust account of the attorney who will be handling the closing or to an escrow company where they are used. *Escrow* is the process where funds are accepted by a third party, who handles both the transfer of funds to the seller and the delivery of the deed to the buyer. In many states, real estate brokers are authorized to handle escrow functions. In some areas of the country, the escrow function is more commonly conducted by attorneys or private escrow companies.

Trust Accounts

The most common depository for earnest money sales and rental deposits as well as for rents and security deposits received when acting as a property manager is the broker's trust account. Even in states where attorneys or escrow companies handle closings, deposits often are made to the trust account of the broker and later transferred to the attorney's trust account or to the escrow company.

Trust accounts must indicate by account name that the money is held in the account for others so as not to be confused with a broker's personal or business funds. Monies from numerous transactions can be kept in the same trust account. Most states require that the trust money be kept in demand deposits (checking accounts) unless directed otherwise by the person making the deposit.

In most states, broker trust accounts also must be in Federal Deposit Insurance Corporation (FDIC)–insured accounts. The FDIC insurance of $100,000 applies to each and every beneficiary, not per account, providing adequate records are kept to show each person's interest in the account. Failure to keep such records would endanger the accounts in the event of a bank's insolvency. A broker who did not keep adequate records therefore would have breached a duty to reasonably protect the funds.

Deposits generally can be kept in interest-bearing accounts when directed to do so by the party depositing the funds. This is fairly common in large commercial and industrial sales where the deposits are significant. Requirements for interest-bearing accounts vary by state but generally accounts must be FDIC insured. Deposits on homes to be built also are frequently placed in interest-bearing accounts because of the long time period of the deposit. The person placing the deposit ordinarily would indicate that all interest earned should accrue to their benefit, unless otherwise agreed. The broker is merely holding the funds for others, so he or she is not entitled to any portion of the interest. When funds are to be held in an interest-bearing account, generally they must be held in separate accounts for each transaction so that interest may be accurately apportioned to the appropriate beneficiary or beneficiaries.

A number of years ago, the broker for a large firm took $10 million out of a trust account and placed the funds in a high-interest, daily money market account with a large stock brokerage firm. The broker designated the account as a trust account. In a hearing to revoke the broker's license, the broker pointed out that no one had been hurt by his actions and the value of the money was being wasted in an interest-free account. The broker was ethically and legally wrong by depositing the funds in an account that was not federally insured. The broker had placed trust money at risk for personal benefit. Had the broker given thought to his actions, he would have seen they could not possibly have passed the test of the Golden Rule. By earning interest on the account, the broker hoped to make a secret profit. Even though he designated the brokerage account as a trust account, the broker had taken the money for his own use. He had effectively embezzled the funds with the intent of returning them, less his profit. His actions were in violation of law and ethics. His license was revoked and he was also subjected to criminal action.

Commingling is the unethical and illegal practice of failure to segregate personal funds from the funds of others. This practice is grounds for revocation of a broker's license. Placing trust funds in a personal account or even in an account intended to be a trust account but not formally designated as such would be considered commingling. It is unethical because it could harm the beneficiary of the funds. As an example, the death, disability or bankruptcy of the broker could result in frozen funds or in some cases the actual loss of the funds. Creditors of the broker could also reach the funds for personal debts of the broker.

Even if a check was only momentarily placed in a personal account for deposit, and the broker then made a deposit from the personal account to the trust account, it is still considered commingling, and the funds were still endangered.

Holding a check uncashed prior to acceptance, when not directed to do so by the buyer, or holding a check uncashed after acceptance, when not directed to do so by the seller, would also be considered commingling in some states.

Holding cash received in your wallet or even your safe could also be considered commingling when it is not deposited in a trust account within a reasonable period of time. In a number of states, deposits must be made to the trust account by the close of the business day following receipt of the deposit.

If a broker placed a deposit check in his or her trust account prior to acceptance of an offer and the offer was rejected, the broker would have to wait until the deposit cleared before returning it. To do otherwise would endanger other parties who have interest in trust monies in the account. If the deposit failed to clear the bank, the broker would have wrongfully used funds of others in prematurely returning the deposit. The trust account balance cannot be less than the beneficiaries' interest in the trust account.

Even if a deposited check was honored by the buyer's bank, the return of the deposit prior to the deposit check's clearing could result in a temporary shortage in the account. Some brokers allow this to happen because they do not want buyers to be angry with them when they cannot promptly return a deposit. To avoid this problem, the broker could simply suggest that the deposited check must be held uncashed until acceptance of the offer. This will also allow buyers to keep their funds in an interest-bearing account until they know they have made a purchase. Brokers should be aware of any state regulations governing this practice.

Because trust account funds are the funds of others and not the broker's, care should be taken to avoid even the hint of any impropriety.

Cash should not be withdrawn from the trust account, because it creates an appearance of impropriety. Withdrawal of cash also increases the risk of loss of the funds and obscures the paper trail of the transaction.

Trust Account Records

The broker must keep adequate records so that not only will it be clear as to interests in trust funds, but will also allow the course of a transaction to be traced. Even though no money was wrongfully appropriated, failure to keep adequate records would still be unethical as the failure could harm the buyer or the seller. The death or disability of the broker, when records are not adequate, could tie up trust funds for a long period of time and also subject the parties to legal expenses.

While there are many good computer programs for trust fund accounting, a paper record should also be kept. Computer data has been known to be erased by accident or by a virus. A proper practice would be to obtain a printout every time a transaction is entered in the computer. Back-up disks also should be used. Reasonable care of trust records would dictate that trust ledgers and computer printouts (and disks) of trust account action be stored in a fire-resistant file or safe.

Whether you use a computer program or a paper-record system, the records should include a general columnar ledger of all trust funds received and paid out showing amount, payor, payee, form of payment, when received and when paid out, check numbers and daily balances. This ledger also is known as a control ledger. A separate record should be kept for each beneficiary or transaction showing the total balance in the account credited to that beneficiary or transaction. When a broker manages properties, there should be a separate record for each property managed. Figure 7.1 is an example of such a record. Often neglected, but important, is a record of trust funds received but not placed in a broker's trust account. These would include transactions where funds are remitted directly to escrow companies or attorneys who are handling the closings as well as deposit checks returned uncashed to buyers when their offers were rejected. Figure 7.2 is an example of a form that can be used for this purpose.

A desired practice that is required in many states involves entering transactions into the records on the day of the transaction and showing the appropriate balance in the account on that date. This reduces the likelihood of an error.

FIGURE 7.1 Separate Record for Each Property Managed

CALIFORNIA ASSOCIATION OF REALTORS

☐

SEPARATE RECORD FOR EACH PROPERTY MANAGED
CALIFORNIA ASSOCIATION OF REALTORS® (CAR) STANDARD FORM

Owner ____________________ Deposit ____________________
Address ____________________ Monthly Rent ____________________
Property ____________________ Commission:
Tenant's Name ____________________ Leases ____________________
Units ____________________ Collection ____________________
Remarks ____________________ Management ____________________

Date	Received From or Paid To	Description	Receipt or Check No.	Amount Received	Date Deposited	Amount Disbursed	Balance

TF-11-3

EQUAL HOUSING OPPORTUNITY
M-SC-MAR-92

FIGURE 7.2   Trust Fund Record Form

RECORD OF ALL TRUST FUNDS RECEIVED — NOT PLACED IN BROKERS TRUST ACCOUNT

CALIFORNIA ASSOCIATION OF REALTORS® (CAR) STANDARD FORM

Date Received	Form of Receipt (Cash, Note, etc.)	Received From	Amount	Description Property or Identification	Disposition of Uncashed Checks or Other Funds Forwarded to Escrow or Principal	Date Forwarded

TRUST FUNDS Including Uncashed Checks Received

TF-11-2

Bank statements should be reconciled with trust records when received. This will allow a bank error or broker error to be ascertained. State licensing laws generally provide a maximum period in which bank statements must be reconciled with the trust account.

Perhaps the most common problem encountered by state real estate agencies are trust fund ledgers that cannot be reconciled with the individual ledger for each beneficiary or transaction. Failure of accounts to balance is, and should be, treated as a serious violation of both trust and law.

Violations of trust fund laws could result in suspension or revocation of a broker's license depending on the severity of the violation. Other consequences could include civil and criminal liability, tax liability and receivership.

The exact accounting format used for records is not really important. What is important is that the records follow accepted accounting practices and that they be complete and in a form that can readily be understood. Figure 7.3 is a sample of a columnar record covering all trust funds received and paid out.

Broker Funds

A broker generally can keep a small amount of broker funds in the trust account. The maximum amount generally is set by state law. By having some broker funds in the account, bank charges can be taken care of. Without broker funds in the account, any bank charges would result in a shortage in the account. Records similar to those kept for each transaction should be kept on broker funds.

Access to Trust Records

Upon request, the broker should give full and complete records of a transaction to an interested party to the transaction.

The broker should cooperate fully with any audit conducted by the state real estate agency or by court order. All trust records should be provided and questions answered honestly and fully. Any stonewalling by refusal, delay or interference with an audit would have to be regarded as unethical conduct, as it would give the perception of a trust account problem that would reflect negatively upon the broker and the entire real estate profession.

FIGURE 7.3 Columnar Trust Funds Record Form

COLUMNAR RECORD OF ALL TRUST FUNDS RECEIVED AND PAID OUT

CALIFORNIA ASSOCIATION OF REALTORS® (CAR) STANDARD FORM

☐

			TRUST FUND BANK ACCOUNT								
			Received				Paid Out				
Date Received	From Whom Received Or To Whom Paid	Description	Amount Received	Cross Ref.	Date of Deposit	xx	Amount Paid Out	Check No.	Date of Check	xx	Daily Balance of Trust Account

TF-11-1

EQUAL HOUSING OPPORTUNITY
M-SC-MAR-92

Disbursement of Funds

When a sale fails, earnest money should not be returned to the buyer or given to the seller without approval of both buyer and seller. To turn the money over to either party could jeopardize rights of the other party. A broker could be civilly liable if a court later determined that the party who received the trust funds was not entitled to them. In some states, brokers are prohibited by law from returning buyer deposits after a purchase contract has been entered into, without the seller's written authorization.

In the event that buyer and seller both claim an interest in funds held in trust, the broker should ethically protect both parties. This can be done through an interpleader action. This action asks the courts to accept the funds and determine who is rightfully entitled to them. Because of the legal costs to the parties, buyer and seller often are willing to arrive at a compromise agreement before an interpleader action becomes necessary. The broker should encourage the parties to negotiate such an agreement, as it would generally be in the best interests of both buyer and seller.

The broker could attempt to mediate the dispute or suggest a mediator to the buyer and seller. Mediation is a process whereby a third party works with the parties in the dispute to help them reach an agreement. Some sales contracts provide for mediation and cover the selection of a mediator.

Real estate sales contracts may provide for binding arbitration if mediation is not successful. The parties agree to be bound by the decision of a third party.

When a transaction has been completed, the broker should promptly disperse funds in accordance with the agreement of the buyer and seller. Unduly holding funds to which others are entitled would be unethical behavior.

Brokers generally use certified or cashier's checks to pay off lenders and other liens as well as for seller proceeds from the sale. This is not really a matter of ethics but is one of good business practice.

The broker should take commission earned from the trust account at closing or as soon thereafter as practical. Leaving earned funds in the trust account after closing would tend to increase the likelihood of an error such as the double withdrawal of commissions.

A number of states designate the maximum period after closing of a transaction within which the broker must withdraw earned commissions from the trust account.

The broker should withdraw trust funds for the entire commission and pay his or her salesperson(s) and cobrokers from the broker's business account. The reason for this is that the listing agreement covers broker's commission, not commission splits. Salespeople employed by the broker are not entitled to trust funds. They are entitled to a share of the commission earned by the broker.

Similarly, when there is a cobroker situation, the broker should give his or her own business check to the cobroker and not pay the cobroker directly from the trust account. An exception would be when the purchase contract specified that the seller would pay the cobroker.

Cooperating brokers and salespeople should ethically be paid on the same day that the broker takes the commission money out of the trust account. The listing broker should not have the use of funds when his or her salespeople and cooperating brokers are denied the same advantage.

Delegation of Trust Fund Authority

A broker may delegate trust fund withdrawals to another party such as an office manager or bookkeeper. The broker should, however, realize that the delegation of such authority carries with it the risk of wrongful appropriation of trust funds. The broker should realize that persons who wrongfully appropriate funds are unlikely to be persons that the broker does not trust. Such persons would not be given the opportunity to wrongfully appropriate funds. Embezzlers tend to be those who are trusted by their employers. Regardless of the number of authorized signators, the broker of record is solely responsible for trust fund accounting.

If a broker delegates trust fund access to others, thus adding an additional risk factor to the beneficiary of such funds, the broker either should be ethically willing and able to make good any loss or should protect the parties by obtaining a fidelity bond covering the wrongful actions by person(s) having access to trust account monies. The amount of the fidelity bond should be sufficient to cover any conceivable loss. In some states, such a fidelity bonding is required by law.

Case Study: "Robbing Peter" To Pay a Contractor

Broker Wu was engaged in property management. Her trust account, which included reserves for expenses, rental security deposits and rents received not yet remitted to owners varied from about $100,000 to almost $1 million, depending on the time of the month.

On a winter morning, with temperatures below freezing, a boiler at a large residential apartment building broke down. A heating contractor indicated that the boiler could not be safely repaired. Broker Wu was able to verify this fact with a heating engineer. By noon, Wu had several estimates for replacement boilers. The only firm that could get on the job that day was also the low bidder. They would only agree to do the job with an $8,200 advance payment to the supply company to pay for the new boiler. While Wu had authority to replace the boiler, there was only $3,100 in the owner's account. The owner was on vacation in Mexico and, despite broker Wu's efforts, could not be located. Rents were due in three days, at which time there would be ample funds to make the repair. Broker Wu made a memo for her file documenting that it was an emergency and that failure to replace the boiler could cause serious damage to the property and also result in tenants breaking leases at a time when the area vacancy rate was high.

Broker Wu wrote a check from the trust fund to the supplier for $8,200 and by midnight of that day the new boiler was installed. Within three days, the rental collections from the property were sufficient to make up for the amount advanced for the boiler.

Analysis

By writing the check out of the trust account for $8,200 when there was only $3,100 credited to the property owner in the account, the broker was in effect giving the owner an interest-free loan of $5,100 from monies held for other owners without the consent of the other owners. This misappropriation of trust funds would be unethical and illegal conduct. The conduct cannot be excused because an emergency existed or because it was only for a few days. The memo explains the "why" of the action, but it was still wrong. It was a case of robbing Peter to pay Paul.

A proper course of action would be for Wu to use company or personal money for the boiler and then receive reimbursement when rents were received. Wu also could obtain a short-term loan. If Wu were unable to make the advance needed, then she could consider offering a discount to tenants if they would pay their rent early. If this was not possible, then the boiler would have to wait until there were sufficient funds.

A patch repair would appear to be an unethical approach, since broker Wu knew that there was a safety problem. A patch repair could result in the endangerment of the tenants as well as potential liability to both the owner and broker Wu. By keeping separate records for each property managed, as shown in Figure 7.1, the broker will always be aware of account balances. This will reduce the likelihood of an accidental misappropriation of funds.

Ethics Questions

1. You are the selling agent on a property listed for sale by ABC Realty. After the sale has closed, you receive a check for your share of the commission from the ABC Realty trust account. The check is returned for insufficient funds. What should you do?

    You should notify ABC Realty of the dishonored check and tell them what you are going to do. Regardless of the explanation given, you should inform ABC Realty that you will be notifying the state real estate agency and you will give them a copy of the dishonored trust account check.

    Even though the dishonor could be an error on the part of the bank and not relate to any negligence or wrongdoing on the part of ABC Realty, the state agency should be notified so that they can investigate and determine if any action is warranted. To fail to do so, even if the check is made good, would put you in a position of knowing of a possible problem and not doing anything about it. This could work to the detriment of members of the public and could negatively reflect on the entire real estate profession. You have an ethical duty to honestly and fully report facts relating to an apparent violation of the law by another licensee. In several states, your duty to report a violation is imposed by law with penalties for those who know of but fail to report a transgression.

    (Note: ABC Realty should have given you a check from their business account, not from their trust account.)

2. Broker Johnson's star salesperson is leaving on vacation and asks for an advance on a sale transaction that is due to be closed later that same day. Broker Johnson writes out a check for the total commission from the trust account. He takes the check to the bank and deposits part of it in his business account and takes cash for the balance, which he gives his salesperson. The sale closes as expected several hours later. Discuss the ethics of Broker Johnson's actions.

    It makes no difference if it was one hour, one day or one month before closing; taking out the commission before the sale was completed is misappropriation of trust funds. It violates a trust.

Broker Johnson could have advanced the salesperson money from his business or personal account.

3. Broker Halprin runs a one-person sales office. His checkbook and deposit slips are his only trust account records. During a particularly hectic period of activity, the broker writes a $5,000 check from his trust account to return a buyer's deposit on an unaccepted offer. A week later, he discovers that he should not have written the check because the buyer's check was in his file. It was not to be cashed unless the offer was accepted. He immediately called his bank and discovered that his $5,000 check had been cashed. He goes to the buyer's bank with the buyer's check but the check could not be cashed because of a stop payment order. What ethical issues are involved?

    Broker Halprin failed to keep adequate trust account records which not only endangered funds of others, it caused funds of others to be wrongfully remitted to a buyer who had no right to the funds.

    While writing the check was an accident, the accident was made possible by a disregard of reasonable protection that would have been afforded by proper record keeping. Failure to keep proper records could therefore be considered unethical conduct. Broker Halprin should immediately reimburse the trust account for the $5,000 that was mistakenly given to the buyer.

    Another ethical problem concerns the attempt to cash the buyer's check. It is clear that the buyer owes broker Halprin $5,000. It is also clear that the buyer, in cashing the broker's check and stopping payment on the check to be deposited, was acting in bad faith in trying to profit at the expense of the broker. However, in trying to cash the buyer's check, Halprin disregarded the instructions accepted with the check. It was not to be cashed unless the offer was accepted. This action was therefore improper.

    An ethical course of action would be for the broker to contact the buyer and ask for the return of the $5,000 that was mistakenly given to the buyer. If the buyer refused, then legal action would be appropriate.

4. Broker Lyons wishes to buy a home listed with her firm. She submits a $350,000 offer for the home. The offer indicates that a $10,000 earnest money payment has been made. The owners reject the offer.

During a subsequent audit of broker Lyons' trust account, the auditor asks about the $10,000 earnest money payment referenced in a file copy of the offer to purchase. Broker Lyons explains that the offer was her offer and if it had been accepted, then she would have been entitled to a commission that greatly exceeded the $10,000 earnest money. Therefore, actually writing a check and showing it in the trust account records was not necessary. Do you agree with broker Lyons?

When a broker indicates in his or her own offer that earnest money has been received, the seller can expect to believe that it is a truthful statement. A seller would be deceived into believing that broker Lyons was showing sincerity in the offer by putting $10,000 at risk should she have backed out of the purchase. It makes no difference that the offer was not accepted. Broker Lyons did not make an earnest money deposit, nor did she intend to do so. Her action must be regarded as unethical. If the seller had acted on the purported earnest money in accepting the offer, the action of broker Lyons could constitute fraud as well.

5. Broker Vukovich wants to make an investment. He visits the loan officer at the bank where he keeps his accounts. He tells the loan officer that he wants a short-term, $250,000 unsecured loan at 1 percent over the prime rate. He also indicates that if the bank does not give him the loan, he is prepared to move his business and trust account to a more cooperative bank. Broker Vukovich points out that there is more than $1 million in his firm's trust account, on which the bank is paying no interest. Discuss the ethics of broker Vukovich's action.

   Broker Vukovich wishes to benefit personally because he controls a trust account. While he did not misappropriate any funds nor did he otherwise endanger the deposits of others, he was attempting to use the trust account as leverage for his personal benefit. If Vukovich simply had asked for a loan and the bank had offered him the loan at an attractive rate of interest, an ethical issue would not have been raised. However, in this case, broker Vukovich has spelled out conditions for a loan and what will happen if it was not granted. While a gray area, the benefits broker Vukovich hoped to receive could amount to a secret profit, in that people making deposits had no knowledge that broker Vukovich intended to shop their funds around for his own benefit. Broker Vukovich also was putting pressure on the bank to make a less-than-prudent loan, which could endanger the funds of depositors. For these reasons, the action of broker Vukovich, while likely legal, should be regarded as unethical.

6. A buyer approaches broker Owens with a proposition. He would buy a home that Owens is offering for sale at $300,000, but wishes to pay cash. The buyer also does not want the broker to make any cash deposit of $10,000 or more, as this would require special bank reporting. Broker Owens agrees and gives the buyer a receipt for $300,000 in cash. Broker Owens puts the money in his safe and makes cash deposits almost daily to his trust account over a period of three months in order to deposit the entire $300,000, after which the sale was then closed. Discuss the ethics of broker Owens' actions.

    In keeping the cash in his safe, even though directed to do so by the buyer, Owens was commingling trust funds. Broker Owens also had a duty to inform the seller as to the nature of the deposit. Owens likely breached this duty.

    Owens could have reasonably deduced the reason the buyer would not wish to have a bank report on the cash. The cash was either money that had not been declared as to taxes or was from illegal activities such as selling drugs. By agreeing to hide the information from the government, broker Owens became an accomplice in a money-laundering scheme that not only was unethical but illegal as well. If the seller knew of broker Owen's actions, the seller could be an accomplice in the money-laundering scheme.

8. Advertising and Ethics

Informed Broker + Honest Property Representation = Fair Advertising

Advertising is an important and necessary element of the real estate profession. It benefits both buyer and seller by disseminating information about available properties that might otherwise be inaccessible to the general public. Misleading advertising, on the other hand, has no place in the real estate business. For example, in Pennsylvania, real estate advertising is considered to be misleading "when taken as a whole there is a distinct possibility that it will deceive the ordinary real estate purchaser, seller, landlord, tenant or other person whom it is intended to influence."

Representing Properties Honestly

Through the years, several horror stories of blatant misrepresentation in the industry have been reported. For example, the Federal Trade Commission once accused a developer of selling virtually worthless land for $7,200 to $8,750 per five-acre parcel. In this case, buyers were told that the land was suitable for homes and for investment. The FTC claimed that the development company went so far in its misrepresentation as to paint in green grass and hang pinecones from the trees on selected lots, which were then photographed for ads. In other cases, developers have claimed that nationally known personalities had purchased land when, in fact, the properties had been given to them as an incentive to endorse the development. Most deceptive advertising is more subtle than in these examples, but regardless of the degree of misrepresentation involved, the end result is the same—readers are deceived.

Bait-and-Switch Schemes

In order to attract customers, some brokers will feature a property that they really don't intend to sell or is not available. Once customers inquire about the property, the broker will tell them either that it has been sold or that the seller has raised the listing price unreasonably. The broker will then show the customer several other properties for sale. This is known as a bait-and-switch scheme, and must be condemned as unethical, deceptive conduct. A similar practice is leaving an ad in the newspaper after the property advertised has been sold. Ads must be canceled as soon as possible after the sale—failure to do so is unethical. Likewise, failing to correct a misprint or misstatement in an ad once it has been discovered would be unethical if the error were misleading. Intentionally "making a mistake" in an ad when the purpose is to increase customer reaction to the ad is pure deceit, even if a correction is published later. In one case, the ad correction was published prior to what was to be the first ad; this led to the conclusion that the mistake was intentional to create interest.

Location

It would be unethical for a broker to advertise that a home is located in a particular neighborhood when, in fact, it is located in a nearby but less desirable area. This is done, once again, to bring buyers into the office—in this case, buyers who are looking for a home in a particular area.

Advertisements often describe locations with phrases such as "20 minutes from the Civic Center." Although such language is common, and the property may be only 20 minutes away during periods of low traffic, the drive may take much longer during morning and afternoon rush hours—when the prospective buyers will normally be making the trip. Using the fastest travel times possible would be deceitful and, therefore, unethical.

Buyer's Agent Ads

Buyer's agent solicitations of buyers should not include such phrases as "you will save" or "guaranteed savings." To indicate that buying through a buyer's agent will cost buyers less is not necessarily true. While savings might be possible, they are not ensured in every case, so such advertising must be regarded as unethical.

Buyer's agent ads that directly or indirectly disparage the activities of seller's agents would be unprofessional, as the spectacle of brokers attacking brokers tends to diminish the public perception of the real estate profession.

Not What It Seems

When preparing ads, using small print or asterisks to clarify either expressed or implied statements could be unethical. For example, ads for many new developments in the Midwest appear to offer low prices, but the small print at the bottom of the ad explains, "All models plus lot and decorating." Apparently, the low price is prominently featured to deceive purchasers.

A common practice is for builders to advertise a very low price in newspapers, signs and brochures. Upon visiting the models, interested home buyers find the models actually priced significantly higher than the advertised prices. They learn that this particular model has "upgraded" tile, carpeting, appliances, cabinets, light fixtures and so on, and thus costs more. Mirrors and wallpaper are "decorator items"—and are not included. While a basic house may be available at the price advertised, the "must-have" features are extra. Using advertising and models in such a way must be regarded as unethical, because the purpose is deception.

Income Properties

Gross and net income figures used in ads for income properties should be checked against recent tax returns. It would be unethical to misrepresent income in general or to advertise the income for a particular year that does not represent the norm. If the gross income advertised is not adjusted by a reasonable vacancy factor and collection loss, it would be unrealistic and could deceive a prospective buyer.

Using overly optimistic expense figures in advertisements is also fraudulent. As a professional, the broker should know if the tax rate has recently changed and should compute annual taxes on this rate—not on old, lower figures. If the utilities costs averaged, say, $3,000 over the past five years, a broker should not quote that figure if the utility rates have been steadily increasing.

Business Opportunities

Unprofitable businesses are often advertised with ads targeted at first-time business owners. Ads often indicate that the business provides a chance to "secure your future" or as a "fantastic opportunity." Advertising failing businesses as if they were profitable when they are more likely to result in the loss of a buyer's life savings must be regarded as unethical. However, it can be proper to advertise location, an advantageous lease and gross income (after verification by the agent) as well as other positive attributes. An agent should not allow a purchase contract to be entered into without the business-buyer having a clear understanding of the business's present financial picture. In the case of an unsophisticated buyer, the agent should recommend that the buyer seek help from a CPA, attorney or other appropriate professional.

If net income is used in an ad, it should be verifiable from the owner's federal income tax returns and not based on oral representations made by the owner. A business owner who wants out often will make statements that cannot be substantiated by the facts. It is fairly easy to prepare a false copy of a tax return. Therefore, if a broker has any doubt as to income claimed, the broker should ask the business owner to show canceled checks made out to the IRS, which would verify that the tax actually was paid. Since a single-year's income could be based on an unusual situation not likely to be repeated, ideally the agent should check prior tax returns for at least three years.

If the net income does not include salaries for the working owner, it could tend to deceive the buyer; therefore, it would be unethical unless the ad indicated that the figure did not include owner salaries. Likewise, it would be misleading to offer net figures for family-run businesses without indicating salary equivalents for any children who may help. As an example, assume that an ad indicates a business generated a $70,000 net profit, but that salary equivalents for business owners and their six children are not shown as expenses. If salaries were paid for their work, the business could be operating at a significant loss. Advertising the net income in this case would be pure deceit.

Use of a disclaimer in advertising that "figures are accurate as to the best of my knowledge and belief," when the broker failed to reasonably check figures does not absolve the broker of liability when accurate figures could have been ascertained.

It would be unethical to advertise gross or net income figures that came from a second set of books (figures other than reported on owner's tax returns). In fact, taking a listing where the agent or the owner will be introducing the buyer to a second set of books would be unethical, as it would condone and likely perpetuate a tax fraud on federal and state governments. It also could subject the agent to criminal penalties.

If an ad indicates the reason for selling the business such as death in the family, retirement or other such reason, this should be confirmed by independent means and approved by the owner.

Verifying Facts

A licensee must be attentive to the facts when writing an ad. For example, if the ad quotes a property's square footage, the broker should check this figure to ensure its accuracy. Failing to verify certain facts and relying simply on an owner's figures could be unethical conduct. Using a figure representing the number of square feet "under roof" is generally intended to mislead, and is therefore unethical. An "under roof" figure usually includes areas such as roof overhang, garages and covered patios, rather than the actual number of square feet of living space in the home or working space in a business. Most multiple listing services have rules as to how square footage should be calculated.

Choosing Your Words Carefully

Colorful language full of vivid adjectives is always recommended for ad copy, but it should not be used to deceive. One developer advertised property that featured "shimmering lakes." In this instance the "lakes" turned out to be two ponds, each covering less than a half-acre.

Advertising terms like *mint condition* and *trouble-free* might be construed as warranties made by the broker. They should not be used unless the broker is willing to guarantee them as being factual. A recent advertisement stated, "Only the highest quality materials were used in the construction and development of these buildings." Any broker making this type of statement has a duty to ascertain whether the level of the construction actually is of the highest quality. To make such a statement without having actual knowledge of the facts could be considered misrepresentation if the property was not as represented.

Phrases such as "good investment" should not be used in ads unless financial statements and business conditions actually indicate that the property is a good investment. Since the broker is considered to be an expert in the field, such a statement, if false, could be considered fraud, not just puffery. Similarly, terms like *bargain*, *below market* and *sacrifice sale* should not be used unless the property's listing price is verifiably below its present market value. Furthermore, it would be unethical to use such language in an ad without the seller's expressed permission, because this sort of advertising implies that the property was listed at too low a price. Likewise, a broker should never advertise "owner asking" a certain price, or "submit an offer," without the owner's permission. This type of advertising suggests that the listed price is not firm and that the owner, whom the listing broker represents, will accept less.

The word *estate* simply means a possessory interest in real property. While any sale of real property could technically be called an estate sale, this term has acquired a popular second meaning: a sale to dispose of property of a deceased owner to settle probate; it also implies the possibility of a bargain. Using "estate sale" in ads for a property not in probate would tend to deceive and therefore must be regarded as unethical even though the description might be technically correct.

Use care in selecting photos, too. Only use photographs in an ad that are representative of the property and have not been altered or taken in a manner that distorts the property to make it look much larger or better than it is. The photo should be as recent as possible and should depict the property as it currently appears, not as it once was.

Representing Your Role and Intentions Honestly

It could be unethical for a broker to advertise that he or she is licensed by the state, as this could imply to readers that other brokers operate without a state license. Some brokers call themselves specialists, using catch phrases such as "Your income property specialist." The term *specialist* denotes *special* training and ability; it would be unethical to advertise oneself as such without having this special expertise. Likewise, brokers should not use a company name that implies that the firm is a nonprofit organization; avoid words such as *bureau* and *institute*.

Salespeople should never advertise under their own names unless their affiliation with the broker is clearly indicated and the broker has approved the ads; in most states, such advertising is a violation of the law. Furthermore, because the broker is responsible for all advertising made in the name of the firm, salespeople should not write and place ads without the broker's review.

Salespersons may, however, properly engage in personal advertising with their names prominently displayed on car signs, name tags, business cards featuring their photograph and so on. Personal advertising is proper and good business practice as long as the broker affiliation is not omitted.

Fees and Commissions

Although it is acceptable for a broker to advertise fees or commission rates, it is unethical for a broker to intimate that he or she provides the same services as other firms for a lower price if, in fact, the services he or she offers are less than would normally be expected. Of course, charging a lower fee than others does not reduce a licensee's responsibility to exercise diligence and to behave in a professional manner at all times.

Buyers and Sellers

Classified ads placed to solicit listings must be honest. Statements such as, "We have buyers, need four-bedroom home," or, "We need nine homes" imply that the broker controls buyers, which may not be the case unless they have exclusive buyer clients.

To obtain listings, some brokers have advertised "free appraisals." This is unethical if the free appraisal consists of nothing more than the usual broker's or salesperson's market evaluation based on the values of comparable properties. If a free appraisal is provided, it should be a written report prepared by a state-certified or licensed appraiser. It would be unethical and possibly illegal to offer a "free" service if that service were contingent on receiving something such as a listing.

Advertising gifts for attending sales presentations appeal to people's greed: They hope to get something for nothing. Such gifts are unprofessional and could reflect negatively on the entire real estate profession. Therefore, offering freebies for attendance must be regarded as unethical conduct even when abusive sales tactics are not used. There is nothing unethical, however, about giving out promotional specialty items or gifts such as pens and calendars that are not tied to attendance at a sales presentation.

Buyer's brokers advertising for buyers should not disparage seller's brokers, nor should seller's brokers disparage buyer's brokers. Negative advertising that tries to run down the competition tends to lower the public's opinion of the entire real estate profession.

Buying Properties

Brokers sometimes advertise that they want to purchase homes. It would be unethical to advertise in this manner if the real purpose of the ad is to obtain listings. Brokers must be honest about their roles and their intentions. If a licensee is advertising to buy or sell property, it is not enough to state, "Contact Mr. Jones"; this would be a blind ad. The licensee is a professional and must never neglect to indicate in any advertisement that he or she is an agent. Even brokers selling their own property should never indicate that property is for sale "by owner" without also indicating that the owner is a real estate licensee. Readers should know that they are dealing with a person who has extensive knowledge in real estate matters. Most states require this disclosure.

Some brokers try to purchase homes using statements such as "We pay up to 100 percent of market value," in their advertising. This statement is misleading—the broker really is saying, "We want to buy for less than fair market value, and the most we will pay is a fair price."

Help-Wanted Ads

Brokers soliciting salespeople in classified ads should only use the "Real Estate Salespeople" category. For example, during recessionary periods of high unemployment in the California aerospace industry, some brokers ran ads that read, "Engineers Wanted," in an attempt to sell them on a new career. Although many engineers may have benefited from the change, the ads were unethical because they recruited individuals under a false pretense.

Firms advertising for salespeople often emphasize only the career's dollar rewards. Although income is important, an extreme emphasis on dollars often attracts only those interested in short-term financial rewards, rather than individuals looking for a personally rewarding career. Besides attracting individuals to the profession who have a "fast buck" attitude, ads emphasizing great financial rewards could give the general public the impression that dollars come before service. This sort of advertising works to the general detriment of the real estate profession and, therefore, is unprofessional. It is also poor business practice, as persons interested solely in immediate financial benefits tend to be very mobile. Because of the time and cost it takes to train an agent, retention of sales agents is critical for a broker's success.

Some firms use glowing phrases such as "Earn commissions of $50,000 to $250,000 per year and more!" Although it is theoretically possible to earn any amount of money selling real estate, if any salesperson with that firm earned less than $50,000 per year, the ad would be misleading, because $50,000 appears to be a minimum. If no salesperson earned more than $250,000 per year, the ad also would be deceptive.

It would be unethical for a broker to advertise that his or her firm offers a "free license preparation course" when, in fact, the future licensee must pay for books or other materials. Any such costs or other conditions to the licensee training should be stated in the ad. In addition, it is deceptive for a broker to advertise that the firm pays a portion of an applicant's prelicensing course if, in reality, the broker pays nothing and simply obtains a reduced rate for the student. Similarly, the broker cannot claim that license training is "free" where the new salesperson gets reimbursed his licensing expense from the broker out of the broker's portion of the commission from his or her first sale. The salesperson may not pass his or her state examination or may never make that first sale.

Fair Housing Advertising

The federal Fair Housing Act states that it is unlawful "to make, print or publish any notice, statement or advertisement with respect to the sale or rental of a dwelling that indicates any preference, limitation or discrimination because of race, color, religion, sex, handicap, familial status or national origin."

It is obvious that phrases such as the following would violate the law: "Blacks Only," "Adults Only," "No AIDS or HIV," "Single-Working Male," "Christian Gentleman," "Married Couples Only" or "Singles Preferred." There are, however, words and phrases that are not so obviously discriminatory. You should be aware that words have different connotations in different geographical areas to different groups. For example, the word "exclusive" might indicate to some minority group members that they are not welcome.

A number of human rights commissions, real estate organizations and newspaper groups have compiled lists of words that are acceptable, as well as words that should be excluded in real estate advertising. You should be aware of guidelines that are available in your area. There has also been some limited clarification by HUD as to words that will not result in legal action by the agency.

The application of the Golden Rule would indicate that you should avoid offending others. Besides being a matter of ethics, violation of both federal and state laws in regard to advertising could result in significant penalties. When in doubt as to the use of a word or phrase, put yourself in the shoes of others who may read your ad. Would you be comfortable responding to the ad?

Supporting a Free Press

At times, real estate firms have withheld advertising from newspapers that have written articles critical of real estate practices. Some brokers have used even more blatantly intimidating tactics. For example, when the *Sacramento Bee* ran a series of stories on discount brokers, one broker wrote to the editor, "I think you should be hanged for the article."

The *Minneapolis Tribune* was once threatened with an industry boycott of advertising when it published a story on a discount real estate agency. These types of actions are unethical because their intent is to interfere with a free press.

Case Study: The Sales Brochure That Was Too Good To Be True

Pineaire is a new 4,800-acre recreational development located in a beautiful, high-desert area of California. The land is from 2,500 to 3,000 feet in elevation and is surrounded by picturesque mountains. Although the nearby mountains are snow-covered, the Pineaire area seldom has snow because of its lower elevation. The area features desert vegetation, while the mountains around have pine forests. The development was designed for recreational vehicles and camping. All-weather roads reach every campsite lot.

Broker Aslam Hossain of Pineaire Realty, who is handling this development, has just designed a new sales brochure that he will use in a mass-mailing campaign to promote the development. The brochure's cover depicts a spectacular snow-covered mountain area dotted with huge pine trees. The photograph was shot on an exceptionally clear day with a 1200mm lens. In small print on the bottom of the cover is the statement, "Picture actually taken from Pineaire property." Inside the brochure, the corners of all the pages are decorated with drawings of pine branches and pinecones. Broker Reynolds felt that this would help tie in the Pineaire image.

A picture of the "Reno Kid," a well-known movie star, is included. It shows Reno making coffee by an open fire. The picture, which was taken at Pineaire, is captioned, "I've pitched my camp at Pineaire. It's my kind of place." Reno, who was paid for the endorsement, does not own property at Pineaire but has said he would actually buy a lot if the company hired him for some planned TV commercials.

One paragraph of the brochure bears the large heading, *Investment Property.* The text goes on to state, "You can invest in your future vacations by buying in Pineaire today." The brochure includes a map showing the major highways and the relationship of Pineaire to various cities and points of interest. Although distances are not shown, Pineaire appears much closer than it actually is to many of the other areas. In small print is the statement, "Map not drawn to scale."

The brochure includes a picture of the new clubhouse for property owners. On first glance it appears as if the developers have spared no expense, because the building looks huge. Actually, it is only 4,000 square feet, but by using a special lens and shooting from the proper angle, the photographer was able to convey the effect that it was massive.

The brochure indicates that water is available. However, water is available, not to each lot, but to the clubhouse, public corral area and washrooms only. The campers could come there to fill their containers.

The brochure features a foldout map of lot sites. Lots are shown in light green, and bridle paths in dark green. In the development, the bridle paths are the many dry riverbeds crossing the property.

The brochure states, "The Pineaire area offers something for everyone. Skiing, snowmobiling, off-road vehicle fun, rock hound paradise, championship golf, tennis, riding, trout fishing." In fact, all of these activities are not located on the property, but most are within a 45-minute drive.

In large letters on the back page is printed, "Special Notice: Pineaire is approved by the U.S. Department of Housing and Urban Development as well as by the California Department of Real Estate."

A coupon enclosed with the brochure states, "A beautiful new vacationland tent designed to sleep six will be given away absolutely free to everyone calling our 800 number for a Pineaire visit. This is a regular $299 value."

Analysis

The name *Pineaire* in itself is misleading. It implies pine trees are on the property when, in fact, none are. When this name is combined with the many pine branches decorating the pages of the brochure, the illusion is increased. Intentional or not, the result is deceptive and unethical.

The cover picture and accompanying statement, "Picture actually taken from Pineaire property," would lead a reasonable person to believe that this was a typical view and that the property was located in snow country. The use of the picture was unethical, since the view shown could not be seen with normal vision from the property, even on a clear day.

Celebrity endorsements are not unethical; however, the Reno Kid's endorsement, "I've pitched my camp at Pineaire. It's my kind of place," conveys the impression that the Reno Kid actually has purchased Pineaire property. Even subtle attempts to mislead must be considered unethical advertising.

The large heading, *Investment Property,* taken alone, could give the impression that the property could reasonably be expected to increase in value. Even though the text indicates that this is not what the advertiser is claiming, the heading could be misinterpreted and should be corrected.

Although the brochure explains that the map is not drawn to scale, it is still misleading. A prospective purchaser could be misled as to the location of Pineaire. This deception is unethical.

The picture of the clubhouse was intended to mislead. This is a blatant deception, and it is, of course, unethical.

A more subtle question arises with the phrase, *water available.* A prospective buyer could reasonably assume that this means that lines are installed so that water could be brought into each lot, since, without a statement to the contrary, a purchaser would naturally assume that water was at the clubhouse, washrooms and corral. The brochure did not clearly indicate that a lot purchaser is expected to go for water with a bucket. Even though the statement was basically truthful, it is still misleading in that it would encourage a prospective buyer to believe other than what was actually the fact.

The foldout map of lot sites was intended to deceive. Light and dark green colors would give a prospective purchaser the impression that the land was lush with vegetation, rather than the parched desert land it is. Labeling dry riverbeds bridle paths might create a vision of the property quite different from the reality.

While the brochure indicates that it is the Pineaire "area" that offers all the recreational activities advertised, it is still confusing. A prospective purchaser, after reading the brochure, would justifiably believe that all of these activities were close to the development, not 45 minutes away. This part of the brochure was intended to deceive and therefore is unethical.

The "special notice" gives the incorrect impression that HUD and the California Department of Real Estate recommend the project. The subdivision was approved for sale, just as every other such subdivision must be. This statement is deceiving, as it appears that there is something special about the approvals in Pineaire's case.

The free tent is a come-on gift to subject prospective buyers to a sales presentation that might use high-pressure tactics. The purpose of a giveaway is to create traffic on the basis of a premium offered rather than on the merits of the property itself. This type of sales method is unprofessional and would raise a serious ethics question if combined with a high-pressure sales presentation.

It would be pure deception if $299 is an inflated value for the tent being offered. Time-share programs in the past have provided unrealistic value for the premiums they offer.

Remember that the real estate profession's greatest visibility is through its advertising. Unethical advertising by one broker reflects on all brokers. A broker therefore has a duty to apply the Golden Rule test to all advertising. Any advertising that does not present a true picture of the property is clearly unethical.

Ethics Questions

1. Henry Fink wants to sell his trophy business. He and his wife have worked full-time on the business during its two-and-a-half years of operation. While the business has shown a profit for the past year, it has not been sufficient to meet the Finks' living expenses. Since they have now exhausted their savings, Henry has taken a teaching job. Last year, the business grossed $180,000, $100,000 of which was from a one-time order of dealer plaques sold to Mr. Fink's uncle, a manufacturer. The Finks would like $40,000 for the business, but you think they are flexible. They would also like enough down to cover the value of machines and inventory—$15,000. After obtaining the listing you place the following advertisement:

   ### Fantastic Potential

   Trophy business—only three years old and already shows over 50 percent return on the total purchase price. A great chance for independence. Owner must sell because of other interests. The confident owner will finance with only $15,000 down. Agent 555-7160.

   What parts of this ad would subject you to criticism? Why?

   The use of potential *is acceptable.* Fantastic, *however, is pure puffery, as the facts do not warrant this description. The business also is not three years old as stated. While it might show a 50 percent return on total purchase price, the profit figure does not consider salaries of the owners, so the 50 percent could be misleading. Without the uncle's business, it is unlikely the business would be profitable. In this case, it is deceptive to indicate that this is a profitable business. Going broke cannot appropriately be called other interests, nor is the owner confident. Overall, the ad implies a thriving business, which is not the case. The ad was written to deceive and is therefore unethical.*

2. A new listing at your office has a large family room converted from the garage. A previous owner did the work, compensating for a lack of skill with zeal. The room has no windows and has electrical outlets on only two walls. You doubt a building permit was ever obtained. A salesperson placed the ad, which reads:

Huge Family Room

Huge family room and three bedrooms in a prestigious West Side location. This won't last long at $97,500. Homebuyers Realty 555-8140.

What, if anything, is wrong with this ad?

The emphasis on the family room is improper, since the city might not allow its continued use. The ad implies that the room can be used for the purpose stated. The agent should have checked with the city or county code enforcement. Moreover, the salesperson should not have placed the ad without broker review and approval.

3. You list a large restaurant and bar for sale at $350,000, including real estate. The present owners have owned and operated the business for 11 years. The owner shows you cash register tapes to support her volume and suggests that you check with her distributors. While the books show only a marginal operation and much lower volume, the owner claims to have made more than $100,000 per year net and states that she will show a serious buyer her second set of books. You place the following advertisement:

Well-Established Restaurant and Bar

Owner reports fantastic net. Includes real estate. $350,000 Submit all offers. Clyde Real Estate 479-6103.

Is there an ethical problem with this ad?

First, since you cannot show the fantastic net, you should make no reference to it. Second, "submit all offers" indicates that the owner will accept less than the listing price; this type of language should not be used without owner approval. Of course you should not indicate any figures other than those reported for tax purposes, and the owner should be aware of this at the time of the listing.

4. You list a new four-family apartment building. The builder rented three of the units for $550 per month, leaving one unit vacant for the owner. Total estimated payments will be approximately $1,600 per month (principal, interest, taxes and insurance). You discover

that the builder gave each tenant one month's free rent to sign a one-year lease. Your ad reads as follows:

Live Rent-Free

Let the other three units of this new, quality-built, four-unit pay all expenses. Call now for more information. 768-4131.

What are the problems with this ad?

An owner cannot live rent-free here. In renting the units, the builder gave the equivalent of a one-twelfth rebate to each tenant, making their true rent approximately $504. Also, maintenance, building utilities and vacancy factor add to the cost. Furthermore, this is a blind ad; it makes no reference to the fact that you are an agent.

5. Gabriel Real Estate included the following in their ads:

Free Portable TV

Everyone listing or buying a home with Gabriel Real Estate during August, our founder's month, will receive, absolutely free, a 12" AC-DC solid-state TV set, including battery pack. This is our way of saying thanks. Gabriel Real Estate 327-8141.

Are there any problems with this ad?

Gabriel has exhibited unprofessional behavior in trying to sell its services on the basis of a giveaway rather than on its quality performance. The free TV offer, however, is not unethical based on the application of the Golden Rule. In most cases, giveaways are legal.

6. You list a 1,200-square-foot, three-bedroom, one-and-a-half–bath home on two and a half acres. Taxes are now $700, which seems low to you compared with taxes on similar properties. You advertise:

Country Estate

Spacious one-story home set among acres of woods and meadows. Low taxes. Doe Realty 874-9841.

What, if anything, is wrong with this ad?

Based on the facts, the term country estate *is not proper. It brings to mind something more than a 1,200 square-foot house. Spacious is stretching the reality quite a bit, and the emphasis on low taxes is not appropriate, since the chances are good that the property will be reappraised after the sale. The phrase "acres of woods and meadows" gives the false impression that the property is much larger than two and a half acres.*

7. Harriet McKell, a new licensee in her first month with Amalgamated Realty, sold six homes, earning her $5,585 in commissions. Amalgamated places the following ad under "Real Estate Salespeople Wanted:"

Be Like Harriet

Harriet McKell earned $5,585 in her first month as a real estate salesperson and is just learning. If income like this interests you, call today to discuss a rewarding future in real estate. Amalgamated Real Estate, where our salespeople come first: 381-7640.

What, if anything, is wrong with this ad?

This ad emphasizes money as the sole reward and would tend to attract people with interests other than a long-term career of serving the needs of the public. The statement "our salespeople come first" shows that Amalgamated Real Estate does not understand its responsibilities under contract and agency law. The firm's first responsibility is, of course, to its principals.

8. Ginsberg Realty made a fantastic sale and trade. They wanted everyone to know what a fine job they had done, so they place the following ad:

How We Beat the IRS

Mr. and Mrs. Simpson couldn't afford to continue to farm their 1,200 acres in Polk County because of increasing taxes. They were too young to retire, and if they sold they would have had to pay a heavy tax burden. Our office found a buyer, Consolidated Investment. We sold Consolidated a 3,200-acre ranch in Oregon for $3.5 million, which they then exchanged tax-free to the Simpsons for their Polk County ranch. We can meet your individual needs also. Ginsberg Realty—The people movers—346-8021.

What, if anything, is wrong with this ad?

The ad would be proper only if Mr. and Mrs. Simpson, Consolidated Investment and the seller of the Oregon ranch consented to it. The prices paid and the reasons for a sale or purchase concern only the parties to the sale and the agent and are not to be broadcast to the general public without permission.

9. Broker Anastasi's company, the Institute of Real Estate Research, advertises that it can find the ideal investment, tailored for each individual, by modern computer search. In fact, it only has a small personal computer which is used for word processing. Property that it sells is owned by Consolidated Land, Inc., which is also owned by broker Anastasi and his family. What are the ethical questions raised?

The use of the words institute *and* research *could lead a person to believe that the firm is nonprofit, which is not the case. The false claim that a computer search will be made is fraud. Also fraudulent is Anastasi's claim that he can find the ideal investment tailored to individual needs, which he has no apparent intention of doing; he wants to sell property from his inventory. In addition, the fact that the broker controls the seller means that broker Anastasi is a principal; his failure to make this disclosure is unethical as well as generally illegal.*

10. A newspaper runs a series of articles about real estate frauds in Florida. All of the major real estate advertisers stop advertising in the newspaper and instead place ads in an area throwaway advertising paper. The paper loses more than 20 percent of its advertising revenue and so starts to run a series of complimentary articles about the advantages of dealing with a broker when buying and selling property.

Is there an ethical problem with the action taken by the major real estate advertisers?

The fact that all of the major firms stopped advertising indicates it was a concerted effort to punish the newspaper, not on the basis of any false stories, but simply because they told about actions of others, which reflected poorly on the industry. The action sent the clear message, "You need us, so get in line or we will put you out of business."

The effect and intent of their actions were to take away the basic rights of a free press and freedom of speech. It was a bullying tactic, which must be considered unethical and should not be condoned.

11. You have just obtained the exclusive sole listing on Sunny Acres, a new residential development built by Omega Construction Company. Omega is a new firm formed by several employees of a major builder in the area. Omega has a special sales incentive—they guarantee in writing that they will buy back any home that they build within 24 months of sale for the full purchase price and will reimburse the buyer's closing costs.

    You promote Sunny Acres as the "No-Risk Home Purchase," and based largely on the guarantee, sell out the development. Within a year, a number of homes develop serious structural problems and the owners want these problems corrected or the guarantee honored. Omega Construction Company declares bankruptcy.

    Is there any ethical problem in this situation as to your conduct?

    You should not have used the builder's guarantee of a buy-back as a sales tool without determining the builder's ability to honor the guarantee. In this case, it was a new builder. You should have suggested the warranty be supported by a bond or insurance coverage of some kind.

12. Popov Popov, a salesperson with Acme Realty, comes up with an effective way to bring in more business. He prepares 5" × 7" cards on one of his listings. He places the cards on bulletin boards at laundromats, supermarkets and social centers:

No Down Payment

3 BR–Fenced Yard

Choice Westside Location

Only $89,500

Contact ALEX POPOV

Your Licensed Local Real Estate Professional

313-2768

PHOTO

Is there any problem with these cards?

The cards are really advertising. Alex Popov fails to indicate his association with Acme Realty. A reader of his cards could assume that Popov is a broker, which is not the case. This deceives the public and must be regarded as unethical. If the broker at Acme Realty did not review these ads, Popov would be guilty of exhibiting unethical conduct, because the broker has responsibility for his ads. Popov could have jeopardized the broker without the broker's knowledge.

By indicating he is licensed, it could give the reader the false impression that all real estate professionals are not licensed, thus wrongfully denigrating the competition. This language does not pass the test of the Golden Rule.

Appendix A

Code of Ethics and Standards of Practice of the National Association of REALTORS®

Code of Ethics and Standards of Practice
of the
NATIONAL ASSOCIATION OF REALTORS®

Effective January 1, 1996

Where the word REALTORS® is used in this Code and Preamble, it shall be deemed to include REALTOR-ASSOCIATE®S.

While the Code of Ethics establishes obligations that may be higher than those mandated by law, in any instance where the Code of Ethics and the law conflict, the obligations of the law must take precedence.

Preamble...

Under all is the land. Upon its wise utilization and widely allocated ownership depend the survival and growth of free institutions and of our civilization. REALTORS® should recognize that the interests of the nation and its citizens require the highest and best use of the land and the widest distribution of land ownership. They require the creation of adequate housing, the building of functioning cities, the development of productive industries and farms, and the preservation of a healthful environment.

Such interests impose obligations beyond those of ordinary commerce. They impose grave social responsibility and a patriotic duty to which REALTORS® should dedicate themselves, and for which they should be diligent in preparing themselves. REALTORS®, therefore, are zealous to maintain and improve the standards of their calling and share with their fellow REALTORS® a common responsibility for its integrity and honor.

In recognition and appreciation of their obligations to clients, customers, the public, and each other, REALTORS® continuously strive to become and remain informed on issues affecting real estate and, as knowledgeable professionals, they willingly share the fruit of their experience and study with others. They identify and take steps, through enforcement of this Code of Ethics and by assisting appropriate regulatory bodies, to eliminate practices which may damage the public or which might discredit or bring dishonor to the real estate profession.

Realizing that cooperation with other real estate professionals promotes the best interests of those who utilize their services, REALTORS® urge exclusive representation of clients; do not attempt to gain any unfair advantage over their competitors; and they refrain from making unsolicited comments about other practitioners. In instances where their opinion is sought, or where REALTORS® believe that comment is necessary, their opinion is offered in an objective, professional manner, uninfluenced by any personal motivation or potential advantage or gain.

The term REALTOR® has come to connote competency, fairness, and high integrity resulting from adherence to a lofty ideal of moral conduct in business relations. No inducement of profit and no instruction from clients ever can justify departure from this ideal.

In the interpretation of this obligation, REALTORS® can take no safer guide than that which has been handed down through the centuries, embodied in the Golden Rule, "Whatsoever ye would that others should do to you, do ye even so to them."

Accepting this standard as their own, REALTORS® pledge to observe its spirit in all of their activities and to conduct their business in accordance with the tenets set forth below.

Duties to Clients and Customers

Article 1

When representing a buyer, seller, landlord, tenant, or other client as an agent, REALTORS® pledge themselves to protect and promote the interests of their client. This obligation of absolute fidelity to the client's interests is primary, but it does not relieve REALTORS® of their obligation to treat all parties honestly. When serving a buyer, seller, landlord, tenant or other party in a non-agency capacity, REALTORS® remain obligated to treat all parties honestly. *(Amended 1/93)*

- **Standard of Practice 1-1**

  REALTORS®, when acting as principals in a real estate transaction, remain obligated by the duties imposed by the Code of Ethics. *(Amended 1/93)*

- **Standard of Practice 1-2**

  The duties the Code of Ethics imposes on agents/representatives are applicable to REALTORS® acting as agents, transaction brokers, facilitators, or in any other recognized capacity except for any duty specifically exempted by law or regulation. *(Adopted 1/95)*

- **Standard of Practice 1-3**

  REALTORS®, in attempting to secure a listing, shall not deliberately mislead the owner as to market value.

- **Standard of Practice 1-4**

  REALTORS®, when seeking to become a buyer/tenant representative, shall not mislead buyers or tenants as to savings or other benefits that might be realized through use of the REALTOR®'s services. *(Amended 1/93)*

- **Standard of Practice 1-5**

  REALTORS® may represent the seller/landlord and buyer/tenant in the same transaction only after full disclosure to and with informed consent of both parties. *(Adopted 1/93)*

- **Standard of Practice 1-6**

  REALTORS® shall submit offers and counter-offers objectively and as quickly as possible. *(Adopted 1/93, Amended 1/95)*

- **Standard of Practice 1-7**

  When acting as listing brokers, REALTORS® shall continue to submit to the seller/landlord all offers and counter-offers until closing or execution of a lease unless the seller/landlord has waived this obligation in writing. REALTORS® shall not be obligated to continue to market the property after an offer has been accepted by the seller/landlord. REALTORS® shall recommend that sellers/landlords obtain the advice of legal counsel prior to acceptance of a subsequent offer except where the acceptance is contingent on the termination of the pre-existing purchase contract or lease. *(Amended 1/93)*

Standard of Practice 1-8

REALTORS® acting as agents of buyers/tenants shall submit to buyers/tenants all offers and counter-offers until acceptance but have no obligation to continue to show properties to their clients after an offer has been accepted unless otherwise agreed in writing. REALTORS® acting as agents of buyers/tenants shall recommend that buyers/tenants obtain the advice of legal counsel if there is a question as to whether a pre-existing contract has been terminated. *(Adopted 1/93)*

Standard of Practice 1-9

The obligation of REALTORS® to preserve confidential information provided by their clients continues after the termination of the agency relationship. REALTORS® shall not knowingly, during or following the termination of a professional relationship with their client:

1) reveal confidential information of the client; or
2) use confidential information of the client to the disadvantage of the client; or
3) use confidential information of the client for the REALTOR®'s advantage or the advantage of a third party unless the client consents after full disclosure except where the REALTOR® is:
   a) required by court order; or
   b) it is the intention of the client to commit a crime and the information is necessary to prevent the crime; or
   c) necessary to defend the REALTOR® or the REALTOR®'s employees or associates against an accusation of wrongful conduct. *(Adopted 1/93, Amended 1/95)*

Standard of Practice 1-10

REALTORS® shall, consistent with the terms and conditions of their property management agreement, competently manage the property of clients with due regard for the rights, responsibilities, benefits, safety and health of tenants and others lawfully on the premises. *(Adopted 1/95)*

Standard of Practice 1-11

REALTORS® who are employed to maintain or manage a client's property shall exercise due diligence and make reasonable efforts to protect it against reasonably foreseeable contingencies and losses. *(Adopted 1/95)*

Article 2

REALTORS® shall avoid exaggeration, misrepresentation, or concealment of pertinent facts relating to the property or the transaction. REALTORS® shall not, however, be obligated to discover latent defects in the property, to advise on matters outside the scope of their real estate license, or to disclose facts which are confidential under the scope of agency duties owed to their clients. *(Amended 1/93)*

Standard of Practice 2-1

REALTORS® shall only be obligated to discover and disclose adverse factors reasonably apparent to someone with expertise in those areas required by their real estate licensing authority. Article 2 does not impose upon the REALTOR® the obligation of expertise in other professional or technical disciplines. *(Amended 1/96)*

Standard of Practice 2-2

When entering into listing contracts, REALTORS® must advise sellers/landlords of:

1) the REALTOR®'s general company policies regarding cooperation with subagents, buyer/tenant agents, or both;
2) the fact that buyer/tenant agents, even if compensated by the listing broker, or by the seller/landlord will represent the interests of buyers/tenants; and
3) any potential for the listing broker to act as a disclosed dual agent, e.g. buyer/tenant agent. *(Adopted 1/93)*

Standard of Practice 2-3

When entering into contracts to represent buyers/tenants, REALTORS® must advise potential clients of:

1) the REALTOR®'s general company policies regarding cooperation with other firms; and
2) any potential for the buyer/tenant representative to act as a disclosed dual agent, e.g. listing broker, subagent, landlord's agent, etc. *(Adopted 1/93)*

Standard of Practice 2-4

REALTORS® shall not be parties to the naming of a false consideration in any document, unless it be the naming of an obviously nominal consideration.

Standard of Practice 2-5

Factors defined as "non-material" by law or regulation or which are expressly referenced in law or regulation as not being subject to disclosure are considered not "pertinent" for purposes of Article 2. *(Adopted 1/93)*

Article 3

REALTORS® shall cooperate with other brokers except when cooperation is not in the client's best interest. The obligation to cooperate does not include the obligation to share commissions, fees, or to otherwise compensate another broker. *(Amended 1/95)*

Standard of Practice 3-1

REALTORS®, acting as exclusive agents of sellers/landlords, establish the terms and conditions of offers to cooperate. Unless expressly indicated in offers to cooperate, cooperating brokers may not assume that the offer of cooperation includes an offer of compensation. Terms of compensation, if any, shall be ascertained by cooperating brokers before beginning efforts to accept the offer of cooperation. *(Amended 1/94)*

Standard of Practice 3-2

REALTORS® shall, with respect to offers of compensation to another REALTOR®, timely communicate any change of compensation for cooperative services to the other REALTOR® prior to the time such REALTOR® produces an offer to purchase/lease the property. *(Amended 1/94)*

Standard of Practice 3-3

Standard of Practice 3-2 does not preclude the listing broker and cooperating broker from entering into an agreement to change cooperative compensation. *(Adopted 1/94)*

Standard of Practice 3-4

REALTORS®, acting as listing brokers, have an affirmative obligation to disclose the existence of dual or variable rate commission arrangements (i.e., listings where one amount of commission is payable if the listing broker's firm is the procuring cause of sale/lease and a different amount of commission is payable if the sale/lease results through the efforts of the seller/landlord or a cooperating broker). The listing broker shall, as soon as practical, disclose the existence of such arrangements to potential cooperating brokers and shall, in response to inquiries from cooperating brokers, disclose the differential that would result in a cooperative transaction or in a sale/lease that results through the efforts of the seller/landlord. If the cooperating broker is a buyer/tenant representative, the buyer/tenant representative must disclose such information to their client. *(Amended 1/94)*

Standard of Practice 3-5

It is the obligation of subagents to promptly disclose all pertinent facts to the principal's agent prior to as well as after a purchase or lease agreement is executed. *(Amended 1/93)*

Standard of Practice 3-6

REALTORS® shall disclose the existence of an accepted offer to any broker seeking cooperation. *(Adopted 5/86)*

Standard of Practice 3-7

When seeking information from another REALTOR® concerning property under a management or listing agreement, REALTORS® shall disclose their REALTOR® status and whether their interest is personal or on behalf of a client and, if on behalf of a client, their representational status. *(Amended 1/95)*

Standard of Practice 3-8

REALTORS® shall not misrepresent the availability of access to show or inspect a listed property. *(Amended 11/87)*

Article 4

REALTORS® shall not acquire an interest in or buy or present offers from themselves, any member of their immediate families, their firms or any member thereof, or any entities in which they have any ownership interest, any real property without making their true position known to the owner or the owner's agent. In selling property they own, or in which they have any interest, REALTORS® shall reveal their ownership or interest in writing to the purchaser or the purchaser's representative. *(Amended 1/91)*

Standard of Practice 4-1

For the protection of all parties, the disclosures required by Article 4 shall be in writing and provided by REALTORS® prior to the signing of any contract. *(Adopted 2/86)*

Article 5

REALTORS® shall not undertake to provide professional services concerning a property or its value where they have a present or contemplated interest unless such interest is specifically disclosed to all affected parties.

Article 6

When acting as agents, REALTORS® shall not accept any commission, rebate, or profit on expenditures made for their principal, without the principal's knowledge and consent. *(Amended 1/92)*

Standard of Practice 6-1

REALTORS® shall not recommend or suggest to a client or a customer the use of services of another organization or business entity in which they have a direct interest without disclosing such interest at the time of the recommendation or suggestion. *(Amended 5/88)*

Standard of Practice 6-2

When acting as agents or subagents, REALTORS® shall disclose to a client or customer if there is any financial benefit or fee the REALTOR® or the REALTOR®'s firm may receive as a direct result of having recommended real estate products or services (e.g., homeowner's insurance, warranty programs, mortgage financing, title insurance, etc.) other than real estate referral fees. *(Adopted 5/88)*

Article 7

In a transaction, REALTORS® shall not accept compensation from more than one party, even if permitted by law, without disclosure to all parties and the informed consent of the REALTOR®'s client or clients. *(Amended 1/93)*

Article 8

REALTORS® shall keep in a special account in an appropriate financial institution, separated from their own funds, monies coming into their possession in trust for other persons, such as escrows, trust funds, clients' monies, and other like items.

Article 9

REALTORS®, for the protection of all parties, shall assure whenever possible that agreements shall be in writing, and shall be in clear and understandable language expressing the specific terms, conditions, obligations and commitments of the parties. A copy of each agreement shall be furnished to each party upon their signing or initialing. *(Amended 1/95)*

Standard of Practice 9-1

For the protection of all parties, REALTORS® shall use reasonable care to ensure that documents pertaining to the purchase, sale, or lease of real estate are kept current through the use of written extensions or amendments. *(Amended 1/93)*

Duties to the Public

Article 10

REALTORS® shall not deny equal professional services to any person for reasons of race, color, religion, sex, handicap, familial status, or national origin. REALTORS® shall not be parties to any plan or agreement to discriminate against a person or persons on the basis of race, color, religion, sex, handicap, familial status, or national origin. *(Amended 1/90)*

Standard of Practice 10-1

REALTORS® shall not volunteer information regarding the racial, religious or ethnic composition of any neighborhood and shall not engage in any activity which may result in panic selling. REALTORS® shall not print, display or circulate any statement or advertisement with respect to the selling or renting of a property that indicates any preference, limitations or discrimination based on race, color, religion, sex, handicap, familial status or national origin. *(Adopted 1/94)*

Article 11

The services which REALTORS® provide to their clients and customers shall conform to the standards of practice and competence which are reasonably expected in the specific real estate disciplines in which they engage; specifically, residential real estate brokerage, real property management, commercial and industrial real estate brokerage, real estate appraisal, real estate counseling, real estate syndication, real estate auction, and international real estate.

REALTORS® shall not undertake to provide specialized professional services concerning a type of property or service that is outside their field of competence unless they engage the assistance of one who is competent on such types of property or service, or unless the facts are fully disclosed to the client. Any persons engaged to provide such assistance shall be so identified to the client and their contribution to the assignment should be set forth. *(Amended 1/95)*

- ## Standard of Practice 11-1
  The obligations of the Code of Ethics shall be supplemented by and construed in a manner consistent with the Uniform Standards of Professional Appraisal Practice (USPAP) promulgated by the Appraisal Standards Board of the Appraisal Foundation.

  The obligations of the Code of Ethics shall not be supplemented by the USPAP where an opinion or recommendation of price or pricing is provided in pursuit of a listing, to assist a potential purchaser in formulating a purchase offer, or to provide a broker's price opinion, whether for a fee or not. *(Amended 1/96)*

- ## Standard of Practice 11-2
  The obligations of the Code of Ethics in respect of real estate disciplines other than appraisal shall be interpreted and applied in accordance with the standards of competence and practice which clients and the public reasonably require to protect their rights and interests considering the complexity of the transaction, the availability of expert assistance, and, where the REALTOR® is an agent or subagent, the obligations of a fiduciary. *(Adopted 1/95)*

- ## Standard of Practice 11-3
  When REALTORS® provide consultive services to clients which involve advice or counsel for a fee (not a commission), such advice shall be rendered in an objective manner and the fee shall not be contingent on the substance of the advice or counsel given. If brokerage or transaction services are to be provided in addition to consultive services, a separate compensation may be paid with prior agreement between the client and REALTOR®. *(Adopted 1/96)*

Article 12

REALTORS® shall be careful at all times to present a true picture in their advertising and representations to the public. REALTORS® shall also ensure that their professional status (e.g., broker, appraiser, property manager, etc.) or status as REALTORS® is clearly identifiable in any such advertising. *(Amended 1/93)*

- ## Standard of Practice 12-1
  REALTORS® shall not offer a service described as "free of charge" when the rendering of a service is contingent on the obtaining of a benefit such as a listing or commission.

- ## Standard of Practice 12-2
  REALTORS® shall not represent that their services are free or without cost if they expect to receive compensation from any source other than their client. *(Adopted 1/95)*

- ## Standard of Practice 12-3
  The offering of premiums, prizes, merchandise discounts or other inducements to list, sell, purchase, or lease is not, in itself, unethical even if receipt of the benefit is contingent on listing, selling, purchasing, or leasing through the REALTOR® making the offer. However, REALTORS® must exercise care and candor in any such advertising or other public or private representations so that any party interested in receiving or otherwise benefiting from the REALTOR®'s offer will have clear, thorough, advance understanding of all the terms and conditions of the offer. The offering of any inducements to do business is subject to the limitations and restrictions of state law and the ethical obligations established by any applicable Standard of Practice. *(Amended 1/95)*

- ## Standard of Practice 12-4
  REALTORS® shall not offer for sale/lease or advertise property without authority. When acting as listing brokers or as subagents, REALTORS® shall not quote a price different from that agreed upon with the seller/landlord. *(Amended 1/93)*

- ## Standard of Practice 12-5
  REALTORS® shall not advertise nor permit any person employed by or affiliated with them to advertise listed property without disclosing the name of the firm. *(Adopted 11/86)*

- ## Standard of Practice 12-6
  REALTORS®, when advertising unlisted real property for sale/lease in which they have an ownership interest, shall disclose their status as both owners/landlords and as REALTORS® or real estate licensees. *(Amended 1/93)*

- ## Standard of Practice 12-7
  Only REALTORS® who participated in the transaction as the listing broker or cooperating broker (selling broker) may claim to have "sold" the property. Prior to closing, a cooperating broker may post a "sold" sign only with the consent of the listing broker. *(Amended 1/96)*

Article 13

REALTORS® shall not engage in activities that constitute the unauthorized practice of law and shall recommend that legal counsel be obtained when the interest of any party to the transaction requires it.

Article 14

If charged with unethical practice or asked to present evidence or to cooperate in any other way, in any disciplinary proceeding or investigation, REALTORS® shall place all pertinent facts before the proper tribunals of the Member Board or affiliated institute, society, or council in which membership is held and shall take no action to disrupt or obstruct such processes. *(Amended 1/90)*

- ## Standard of Practice 14-1
  REALTORS® shall not be subject to disciplinary proceedings in more than one Board of REALTORS® or affiliated institute, society or council in which they hold membership with respect to alleged violations of the Code of Ethics relating to the same transaction or event. *(Amended 1/95)*

- ## Standard of Practice 14-2
  REALTORS® shall not make any unauthorized disclosure or dissemination of the allegations, findings, or decision

developed in connection with an ethics hearing or appeal or in connection with an arbitration hearing or procedural review. *(Amended 1/92)*

- ### Standard of Practice 14-3
  REALTORS® shall not obstruct the Board's investigative or disciplinary proceedings by instituting or threatening to institute actions for libel, slander or defamation against any party to a professional standards proceeding or their witnesses. *(Adopted 11/87)*

- ### Standard of Practice 14-4
  REALTORS® shall not intentionally impede the Board's investigative or disciplinary proceedings by filing multiple ethics complaints based on the same event or transaction. *(Adopted 11/88)*

Duties to REALTORS®

Article 15

REALTORS® shall not knowingly or recklessly make false or misleading statements about competitors, their businesses, or their business practices. *(Amended 1/92)*

Article 16

REALTORS® shall not engage in any practice or take any action inconsistent with the agency of other REALTORS®.

- ### Standard of Practice 16-1
  Article 16 is not intended to prohibit aggressive or innovative business practices which are otherwise ethical and does not prohibit disagreements with other REALTORS® involving commission, fees, compensation or other forms of payment or expenses. *(Adopted 1/93, Amended 1/95)*

- ### Standard of Practice 16-2
  Article 16 does not preclude REALTORS® from making general announcements to prospective clients describing their services and the terms of their availability even though some recipients may have entered into agency agreements with another REALTOR®. A general telephone canvass, general mailing or distribution addressed to all prospective clients in a given geographical area or in a given profession, business, club, or organization, or other classification or group is deemed "general" for purposes of this standard.

  Article 16 is intended to recognize as unethical two basic types of solicitations:

  First, telephone or personal solicitations of property owners who have been identified by a real estate sign, multiple listing compilation, or other information service as having exclusively listed their property with another REALTOR®; and

  Second, mail or other forms of written solicitations of prospective clients whose properties are exclusively listed with another REALTOR® when such solicitations are not part of a general mailing but are directed specifically to property owners identified through compilations of current listings, "for sale" or "for rent" signs, or other sources of information required by Article 3 and Multiple Listing Service rules to be made available to other REALTORS® under offers of subagency or cooperation. *(Amended 1/93)*

- ### Standard of Practice 16-3
  Article 16 does not preclude REALTORS® from contacting the client of another broker for the purpose of offering to provide, or entering into a contract to provide, a different type of real estate service unrelated to the type of service currently being provided (e.g., property management as opposed to brokerage). However, information received through a Multiple Listing Service or any other offer of cooperation may not be used to target clients of other REALTORS® to whom such offers to provide services may be made. *(Amended 1/93)*

- ### Standard of Practice 16-4
  REALTORS® shall not solicit a listing which is currently listed exclusively with another broker. However, if the listing broker, when asked by the REALTOR®, refuses to disclose the expiration date and nature of such listing; i.e., an exclusive right to sell, an exclusive agency, open listing, or other form of contractual agreement between the listing broker and the client, the REALTOR® may contact the owner to secure such information and may discuss the terms upon which the REALTOR® might take a future listing or, alternatively, may take a listing to become effective upon expiration of any existing exclusive listing. *(Amended 1/94)*

- ### Standard of Practice 16-5
  REALTORS® shall not solicit buyer/tenant agency agreements from buyers/tenants who are subject to exclusive buyer/tenant agency agreements. However, if a buyer/tenant agent, when asked by a REALTOR®, refuses to disclose the expiration date of the exclusive buyer/tenant agency agreement, the REALTOR® may contact the buyer/tenant to secure such information and may discuss the terms upon which the REALTOR® might enter into a future buyer/tenant agency agreement or, alternatively, may enter into a buyer/tenant agency agreement to become effective upon the expiration of any existing exclusive buyer/tenant agency agreement. *(Adopted 1/94)*

- ### Standard of Practice 16-6
  When REALTORS® are contacted by the client of another REALTOR® regarding the creation of an agency relationship to provide the same type of service, and REALTORS® have not directly or indirectly initiated such discussions, they may discuss the terms upon which they might enter into a future agency agreement or, alternatively, may enter into an agency agreement which becomes effective upon expiration of any existing exclusive agreement. *(Amended 1/93)*

- ### Standard of Practice 16-7
  The fact that a client has retained a REALTOR® as an agent in one or more past transactions does not preclude other REALTORS® from seeking such former client's future business. *(Amended 1/93)*

- ### Standard of Practice 16-8
  The fact that an agency agreement has been entered into with a REALTOR® shall not preclude or inhibit any other REALTOR® from entering into a similar agreement after the expiration of the prior agreement. *(Amended 1/93)*

- ### Standard of Practice 16-9
  REALTORS®, prior to entering into an agency agreement, have an affirmative obligation to make reasonable efforts to

determine whether the client is subject to a current, valid exclusive agreement to provide the same type of real estate service. *(Amended 1/93)*

- ### Standard of Practice 16-10

  REALTORS®, acting as agents of buyers or tenants, shall disclose that relationship to the seller/landlord's agent at first contact and shall provide written confirmation of that disclosure to the seller/landlord's agent not later than execution of a purchase agreement or lease. *(Amended 1/93)*

- ### Standard of Practice 16-11

  On unlisted property, REALTORS® acting as buyer/tenant agents shall disclose that relationship to the seller/landlord at first contact for that client and shall provide written confirmation of such disclosure to the seller/landlord not later than execution of any purchase or lease agreement.

  REALTORS® shall make any request for anticipated compensation from the seller/landlord at first contact. *(Amended 1/93)*

- ### Standard of Practice 16-12

  REALTORS®, acting as agents of sellers/landlords or as subagents of listing brokers, shall disclose that relationship to buyers/tenants as soon as practicable and shall provide written confirmation of such disclosure to buyers/tenants not later than execution of any purchase or lease agreement. *(Amended 1/93)*

- ### Standard of Practice 16-13

  All dealings concerning property exclusively listed, or with buyer/tenants who are exclusively represented shall be carried on with the client's agent, and not with the client, except with the consent of the client's agent. *(Adopted 1/93)*

- ### Standard of Practice 16-14

  REALTORS® are free to enter into contractual relationships or to negotiate with sellers/landlords, buyers/tenants or others who are not represented by an exclusive agent but shall not knowingly obligate them to pay more than one commission except with their informed consent. *(Amended 1/94)*

- ### Standard of Practice 16-15

  In cooperative transactions REALTORS® shall compensate cooperating REALTORS® (principal brokers) and shall not compensate nor offer to compensate, directly or indirectly, any of the sales licensees employed by or affiliated with other REALTORS® without the prior express knowledge and consent of the cooperating broker.

- ### Standard of Practice 16-16

  REALTORS®, acting as subagents or buyer/tenant agents, shall not use the terms of an offer to purchase/lease to attempt to modify the listing broker's offer of compensation to subagents or buyer's agents nor make the submission of an executed offer to purchase/lease contingent on the listing broker's agreement to modify the offer of compensation. *(Amended 1/93)*

- ### Standard of Practice 16-17

  REALTORS® acting as subagents or as buyer/tenant agents, shall not attempt to extend a listing broker's offer of cooperation and/or compensation to other brokers without the consent of the listing broker. *(Amended 1/93)*

- ### Standard of Practice 16-18

  REALTORS® shall not use information obtained by them from the listing broker, through offers to cooperate received through Multiple Listing Services or other sources authorized by the listing broker, for the purpose of creating a referral prospect to a third broker, or for creating a buyer/tenant prospect unless such use is authorized by the listing broker. *(Amended 1/93)*

- ### Standard of Practice 16-19

  Signs giving notice of property for sale, rent, lease, or exchange shall not be placed on property without consent of the seller/landlord. *(Amended 1/93)*

Article 17

In the event of a contractual dispute between REALTORS® associated with different firms, arising out of their relationship as REALTORS®, the REALTORS® shall submit the dispute to arbitration in accordance with the regulations of their Board or Boards rather than litigate the matter.

In the event clients of REALTORS® wish to arbitrate contractual disputes arising out of real estate transactions, REALTORS® shall arbitrate those disputes in accordance with the regulations of their Board, provided   the clients agree to be bound by the decision. *(Amended 1/94)*

- ### Standard of Practice 17-1

  The filing of litigation and refusal to withdraw from it by REALTORS® in an arbitrable matter constitutes a refusal to arbitrate. *(Adopted 2/86)*

- ### Standard of Practice 17-2

  Article 17 does not require REALTORS® to arbitrate in those circumstances when all parties to the dispute advise the Board in writing that they choose not to arbitrate before the Board. *(Amended 1/93)*

- ### Standard of Practice 17-3

  REALTORS®, when acting solely as principals in a real estate transaction, are not obligated to arbitrate disputes with other REALTORS® absent a specific written agreement to the contrary. *(Adopted 1/96)*

The Code of Ethics was adopted in 1913. Amended at the Annual Convention in 1924, 1928, 1950, 1951, 1952, 1955, 1956, 1961, 1962, 1974, 1982, 1986, 1987, 1989, 1990, 1991, 1992, 1993, 1994 and 1995.

Explanatory Notes

The reader should be aware of the following policies which have been approved by the Board of Directors of the National Association:

In filing a charge of an alleged violation of the Code of Ethics by a REALTOR®, the charge must read as an alleged violation of one or more Articles of the Code. Standards of Practice may be cited in support of the charge.

The Standards of Practice serve to clarify the ethical obligations imposed by the various Articles and supplement, and do not substitute for, the Case Interpretations in **Interpretations of the Code of Ethics**.

Modifications to existing Standards of Practice and additional new Standards of Practice are approved from time to time. Readers are cautioned to ensure that the most recent publications are utilized.

Appendix B

California Code of Ethics and Professional Conduct and Suggestions for Professional Conduct [Regulations of the Real Estate Commissioner (Chapter 6, Title 10, California Administrative Code)]

Regulations of the Real Estate Commissioner
(Chapter 6, Title 10, California Administrative Code)

Article 11 Code of Ethics and Professional Conduct

§2785. Professional Conduct. In order to enhance the professionalism of the California real estate industry, and maximize protection for members of the public dealing with real estate licensees, whatever their area of practice, the following standards of professional conduct and business practices are adopted.

(a) **Unlawful Conduct in Sale, Lease and Exchange Transactions.** Licensees when performing acts within the meaning of section 10131(a) of the Business and Professions Code shall not engage in conduct which would subject the licensee to adverse action, penalty or discipline under sections 10176 or 10177 of the Business and Professions Code including, but not limited to, the following acts and omissions:

    (1) Knowingly making a substantial misrepresentation of the likely value of real property to:

        (A) Its owner either for the purpose of securing a listing or for the purpose of acquiring an interest in the property for the licensee's own account.

        (B) A prospective buyer for the purpose of inducing the buyer to make an offer to purchase the real property.

    (2) Representing to an owner of real property when seeking a listing that the licensee has obtained a bona fide written offer to purchase the property, unless at the time of the representation the licensee has possession of a bona fide written offer to purchase.

    (3) Stating or implying to an owner of real property during listing negotiations that the licensee is precluded by law, by regulation, or by the rules of any organization, other than the broker firm seeking the listing, from charging less than the commission or fee quoted to the owner by the licensee.

    (4) Knowingly making substantial misrepresentations regarding the licensee's relationship with an individual broker, corporate broker, or franchised brokerage company or that entity's/person's responsibility for the licensee's activities.

    (5) Knowingly underestimating the probable closing costs in a communication to the prospective buyer or seller of real property in order to induce that person to make or to accept an offer to purchase the property.

    (6) Knowingly making a false or misleading representation to the seller of real property as to the form, amount and/or treatment of a deposit toward the purchase of the property made by an offeror.

    (7) Knowingly making a false or misleading representation to a seller of real property, who has agreed to finance all or part of a purchase price by carrying back a loan, about a buyer's ability to repay the loan in accordance with its terms and conditions.

    (8) Making an addition to an modification of the terms of an instrument previously signed or initialed by a party to a transaction without the knowledge and consent of the party.

(9) A representation made as a principal or agent to a prospective purchaser of a promissory note secured by real property about the market value of the securing property without a reasonable basis for believing the truth and accuracy of the representation.

(10) Knowingly making a false or misleading representation or representing, without a reasonable basis for believing its truth, the nature and/or condition of the interior or exterior features of a property when soliciting an offer.

(11) Knowingly making a false or misleading representation or representing, without a reasonable basis for believing its truth, the size of a parcel, square footage of improvements or the location of the boundary lines of real property being offered for sale, lease or exchange.

(12) Knowingly making a false or misleading representation or representing to a prospective buyer or lessee of real property, without a reasonable basis to believe its truth, that the property can be used for certain purposes with the intent of inducing the prospective buyer or lessee to acquire an interest in the real property.

(13) When acting in the capacity of an agent in a transaction for the sale, lease or exchange of real property, failing to disclose to a prospective purchaser or lessee facts known to the licensee materially affecting the value or desirability of the property, when the licensee has reason to believe that such facts are not known to nor readily observable by a prospective purchaser or lessee.

(14) Willfully failing, when acting as a listing agent, to present or cause to be repre-

sented to the owner of the property any written offer to purchase received prior to the closing a sale, unless expressly instructed by the owner not to present such an offer, or unless expressly instructed by the owner not to present such an offer, or unless the offer is patently frivolous.

(15) When acting as the listing agent, presenting competing written offers to purchase real property to the owner in such a manner as to include the owner to accept the offer which will provide the greatest compensation to the listing broker without regard to the benefits, advantages and/or disadvantages to the owner.

(16) Failing to explain to the parties or prospective parties to a real estate transaction for whom the licensee is acting as an agent the meaning and probable significance of a contingency in an offer or contract that the licensee knows or reasonably believes may affect the closing date of the transaction, or the timing of the vacating of the property by the seller or its occupancy by the buyer.

(17) Failing to disclose to the seller of real property in a transaction in which the licensee is an agent for the seller the nature and extent of any direct or indirect interest that the licensee expects to acquire as a result of the sale. The prospective purchase of the property by a person related to the licensee by blood or marriage, purchase by an entity in which the licensee has an ownership interest, or purchase by any other person with whom the licensee occupies a special relationship where there is a reasonable probability that the licensee could be indirectly acquir-

ing an interest in the property shall be disclosed to the seller.

(18) Failing to disclose to the buyer of real property in a transaction in which the licensee is an agent for the buyer the nature and extent of a licensee's direct or indirect ownership interest in such real property. The direct or indirect ownership interest in the property by a person related to the licensee by blood or marriage, by an entity in which the licensee has an ownership interest, or by any other person with whom the licensee occupies a special relationship shall be disclosed to the buyer.

(19) Failing to disclose to a principal for whom the licensee is acting as an agent any significant interest the licensee has in a particular entity when the licensee recommends the use of the services or products of such entity.

(b) **Unlawful Conduct When Soliciting, Negotiating or Arranging a Loan Secured by Real Property or the Sale of a Promissory Note Secured by Real Property.** Licensees when performing acts within the meaning of subdivision (d) or (e) of section 10131 of the Business and Professions Code shall not violate any of the applicable provisions of subdivision (a), or act in a manner which would subject the licensee to adverse action, penalty or discipline under sections 10176 and 10177 of the Business and Professions Code including, but not limited to, the following acts and omissions:

(1) Knowingly misrepresenting to a prospective borrower of a loan to be secured by real property or to an assignor/endorser of a promissory note secured by real property that there is an existing lender willing to make the loan or that there is a purchaser for the note, for the purpose of inducing the borrower or assignor/endorser to utilize the services of the licensee.

(2)(A) Knowingly making a false or misleading representation to a prospective lender or purchaser of a loan secured directly or collaterally by real property about a borrower's ability to repay the loan in accordance with its terms and conditions;

(B) Failing to disclose to a prospective lender or note purchaser information about the prospective borrower's identity, occupation, employment, income and credit data as represented to the broker by the prospective borrower;

(C) Failing to disclose information known to the broker relative to the ability of the borrower to meet his or her potential or existing contractual obligations under the note or contract including information known about the borrower's payment history on an existing note, whether the note is in default or the borrower in bankruptcy.

(3) Knowingly underestimating the probable closing costs in a communication to a prospective borrower or lender of a loan to be secured by a lien on real property for the purpose of inducing the borrower or lender to enter into the loan transaction.

(4) When soliciting a prospective lender to make a loan to be secured by real property, falsely representing or representing without a reasonable basis to believe its truth, the priority of the security, as a lien against the real prop-

erty securing the loan, i.e., a first, second or third deed of trust.

(5) Knowingly misrepresenting in any transaction that a specific service is free when the licensee knows or has a reasonable basis to know that it is covered by a fee to be charged as part of the transaction.

(6) Knowingly making a false or misleading representation to a lender or assignee/endorsee of a lender of a loan secured directly or collaterally by a lien on real property about the amount and treatment of loan payments, including loan payoffs, and the failure to account to the lender or assignee/endorsee of a lender as to the disposition of such payments.

(7) When acting as a licensee in a transaction for the purpose of obtaining a loan, and in receipt of an "advance fee" from the borrower for this purpose, the failure to account to the borrower for the disposition of the "advance fee."

(8) Knowingly making false or misleading representation about the terms and conditions of a loan to be secured by a lien on real property when soliciting a borrower or negotiating the loan.

(9) Knowingly making a false or misleading representation or representing, without a reasonable basis for believing its truth, when soliciting a lender or negotiating a loan to be secured by a lien on real property about the market value of the securing real property, the nature and/or condition of the interior or exterior features of the securing real property, its size or the square footage of any improvements on the securing real property.

Note: The Real Estate Commissioner has issued *Suggestions for Professional Conduct in Sale, Lease and Exchange Transactions and Suggestions for Professional Conduct When Negotiating or Arranging Loans Secured by Real Property or Sale of a Promissory Note Secured by Real Property.*

The purpose of the Suggestions is to encourage real estate licensees to maintain a high level of ethics and professionalism in their business practices when performing acts for which a real estate license is required.

The Suggestions are not intended as statements of duties imposed by law nor as grounds for disciplinary action by the Department of Real Estate, but as suggestions for elevating the professionalism of real estate licensees.

As part of the effort to promote ethical business practices of real estate licensees, the Real Estate Commissioner has issued the following Suggestions for Professional Conduct as a companion to the *Code of Professional Conduct* (Section 2785, Title 10, California Code of Regulations):

(a) *Suggestions for Professional Conduct in Sale, Lease and Exchange Transactions.* In order to maintain a high level of ethics and professionalism in their business practices, real estate licensees are encouraged to adhere to the following suggestions in conducting their business activities:

   (1) Aspire to give a high level of competent, ethical and quality service to buyers and sellers in real estate transactions.

   (2) Stay in close communication with clients or customers to ensure that questions are promptly answered and all significant events or problems in a

transaction are conveyed in a timely manner.

(3) Cooperate with the California Department of Real Estate's enforcement of, and report to that Department evident violations of, the Real Estate Law.

(4) Use care in the preparation of any advertisement to present an accurate picture or message to the reader, viewer or listener.

(5) Submit all written offers in a prompt and timely manner.

(6) Keep oneself informed and current on factors affecting the real estate market in which the licensee operates as an agent.

(7) Make a full, open and sincere effort to cooperate with other licensees, unless the principal has instructed the licensee to the contrary.

(8) Attempt to settle disputes with other licensees through mediation or arbitration.

(9) Advertise or claim to be an expert in an area of specialization in real estate brokerage activity, e.g., appraisal, property management, industrial siting, mortgage loan, etc., only if the licensee has had special training, preparation or experience in such areas.

(10) Strive to provide equal opportunity for quality housing and a high level of service to all persons regardless of race, color, sex, religion, ancestry, physical handicap, marital status or national origin.

(11) Base opinions of value, whether for the purpose of advertising or promoting real estate brokerage business, upon documented objective data.

(12) Make every attempt to comply with these Suggestions for Professional Conduct and the Code of Ethics of any organized real estate industry group of which the licensee is a member.

(13) Obtain written instructions from both parties to a transaction prior to disbursing a purchase money deposit to a party.

(b) *Suggestions for Professional Conduct When Negotiating or Arranging Loans Secured by Real Property or Sale of a Promissory Note Secured by Real Property.* In order to maintain a high level of ethics and professionalism in their business practices when performing acts within the meaning of subdivision (d) and (e) of Section 10131 and Sections 10131.1 and 10131.2 of the Business and Professions Code, real estate licensees are encouraged to adhere to the following suggestions, in addition to any applicable provisions of subdivision (a), in conducting their business activities:

(1) Aspire to give a high level of competent, ethical and quality service to borrowers and lenders in loan transactions secured by real estate.

(2) Stay in close communication with borrowers and lenders to ensure that reasonable questions are promptly answered and all significant events or problems in a loan transaction are conveyed in a timely manner.

(3) Keep oneself informed and current on factors affecting the real estate loan market in which the licensee acts as an agent.

(4) Advertise or claim to be an expert in an area of specialization in real estate mortgage loan transactions only if the licensee has had special training, preparation or experience in such area.

(5) Strive to provide equal opportunity for quality mortgage loan services and a high level of service to all borrowers or lenders regardless of race, color, sex, religion, ancestry, physical handicap, marital status or national origin.

(6) Base opinions of value in a loan transaction, whether for the purpose of advertising or promoting real estate mortgage loan brokerage business, on documented objective data.

(7) Respond to reasonable inquiries of a principal as to the status or extent of efforts to negotiate the sale of an existing loan.

(8) Respond to reasonable inquiries of a borrower regarding the net proceeds available from a loan arranged by the licensee.

(9) Make every attempt to comply with the standards of professional conduct and the code of ethics of any organized mortgage loan industry group of which the licensee is a member.

The conduct suggestions set forth in subsections (a) and (b) are not intended as statements of duties imposed by law nor as grounds for disciplinary action by the Department of Real Estate, but as guidelines for elevating the professionalism of real estate licensees.

Note: Authority cited: Section 10080, Business and Professions Code.

Reference: Sections 10176 and 10177, Business and Professions Code.

Index

Index